COUNTER CULTURE

ILR Press

An Imprint of

CORNELL UNIVERSITY PRESS

ITHACA AND LONDON

COUNTER

THE AMERICAN COFFEE SHOP WAITRESS

CULTURE

CANDACY A. TAYLOR

First published 2009 by Cornell University Press

First printing, Cornell Paperbacks, 2009

Printed in China

Library of Congress Cataloging-in-Publication Data
Taylor, Candacy A.
   Counter culture : the American coffee shop waitress / Candacy A. Taylor.
    p. cm.
   Includes bibliographical references.
   ISBN 978-0-8014-7440-8 (pbk. : alk. paper)
  1. Waitresses—United States. 2. Coffee shops—United States—Employees.
3. Diners (Restaurants)—United States—Employees. 4. Table service—United
States. I. Title.
   HD6073.H82U5 2009
   647.95—dc22   2009004248

Cornell University Press strives to use environmentally responsible suppliers and materials to the fullest extent possible in the publishing of its books. Such materials include vegetable-based, low-VOC inks and acid-free papers that are recycled, totally chlorine-free, or partly composed of nonwood fibers. For further information, visit our website at www.cornellpress.cornell.edu.

Paperback printing   10 9 8 7 6 5 4 3 2 1

This book is dedicated to Baba, Mom, Ron, Aimeé, and to the women it celebrates

Contents

Acknowledgments

This book would not have been possible without the lifelong support of my mother, Carol Burford. After every rejection she reminded me how far I had come and reassured me that success was just over the horizon. In those times when I did receive recognition—a front-page article about my project in the arts section of a major newspaper, a grant award, or when Southwest Airlines included my exhibition in their top-ten list of things to see in the United States—Mom was there to share in the celebration. We treated ourselves to nice hotels where we could relax, order room service, and knit. She also helped me interview the waitresses. Although I've had several interns over the years, no one could match my mother's genuine desire to do the job right. Her meticulous organization skills ensured that we arrived on time to every appointment, with all of the digital equipment charged up and ready to go; and more importantly, the waitresses liked her, which helped immensely when the time came to sign the consent form.

I am deeply grateful for the endless support and love from Jaimie Kiggins, Tatiana Brennan, Christel Schmidt, Hilary Reed, Krista and Doug Alexander, Mike Farruggia, Clifford Richmond, Mike Miller, Fred Schwab, Jeff and Patti Cowans, David A. M. Goldberg, Elwyn Crawford, Deborah Munk, Cheri Wong, the Deegans, Joyce VanHorn, Beth and Rich Lasky, Charice Silverman, Maurice Saah, Andrea Clardy, Vicki Schmall, Patrick Arbore, Linda Willhard, and Jason Teplitsky at Blowfish Sushi.

Thank you to the following photographers, filmmakers, artists, and writers for their encouragement, information, and advice: Rick Nahmais, Adger Cowans, Roland L. Freeman, Ryan Farnau, Joseph Blum, Peter Samuels, Gary Gladstone, Suzanne Onodera, Rosemary Allen, Nellie King Solomon, Susan Stern, Emiko Omori, David L. Brown, Jay Wood, Opal Palmer Adisa, Richard Gutman, Jewelle Gomez, Jeff Howe, Julie Winokur, Sarah Mahoney, Alan Kaufman, Bill Woods, Matt Wagner, Michael W. Dean, and Nathan Gebhard.

Thanks to the following who offered their time and technical expertise to the project: Sterling Storm, Kathleen Sullivan, Dorothy Sue Cobble, Alison Owings, Sarah Rolph, Eileen Whitfield, Tom DeCarlo, Christine Lynn Harris, my former agent Jim McCarthy, Sharon Anderson, Joe Morris, Robert Day, Ronna Molson, Christine Waring, Emily Hughes, Sophia Renn, Katie Piccagli, and Ron Turner at Last Gasp Publishing.

Thanks to the following art administrators and media producers: K. C. Murphy Thompson, Ginny Brush, and Rita Ferri at the Santa Barbara Arts Commission; Rupert Jenkins and Carol Marie Daniels at the San Francisco Arts Commission; Ralph Lewin and Maura Hurley at the California Council for the Humanities; Deborah and

Jim Gangwer and Doreen Schmid at Subject Matters; Neil Harvey at Copia, Susan Sherwood at the San Francisco State University Labor Archives and Research Center, Phyllis Owens at *Weekend America* (NPR). And special thanks to Ben Sandler for hanging my first photo exhibition of the waitress project.

I am indebted to the following educators who inspired and challenged me to create meaningful work: Robert Bechtle, Fred Kling, Paul Pratchenko, Melanie Wise, Mitchell Schwarzer, John Laskey, Mabel Wilson, Barry Katz, Lydia Matthews, and Mark Bartlett.

This book would not have been possible without the financial support of Margaret Bolton, Carol and Ron Burford, the California Council for the Humanities and the Kentucky Oral History Commission.

My deepest appreciation and gratitude to my editor, Fran Benson—her enthusiasm, adoration, and tireless support of my work motivated me to work harder than I ever have in my life.

And finally, thanks to all of the waitresses who generously donated their time and fearlessly trusted me with their stories.

COUNTER CULTURE

TRUCK INN, ROUTE 80, SPARKS, NEVADA

Introduction

Since 2001, I have traveled over twenty-six thousand miles criss-crossing the United States, taking photographs and collecting stories of older career waitresses. The idea came to me while waitressing in a sushi restaurant in San Francisco. After a busy Friday night, I sat down in the back with the other servers to count my tips. The back table was a place to do paperwork, divide up money to tip out coworkers, and to relive all the drama of the evening. We swapped stories about our futile attempts to reason with irrational customers, we commiserated about the great effort it took to get the food out of the kitchen, and then we would suddenly remember orders we never placed. While eating our late-night dinners and balancing our sales reports we dreamed about what we were going to do with our lives after we left waiting tables for our true calling. We complained about how tired we were—our feet throbbed, our legs ached, and our arms were sore. On that Friday night I thought to myself, if *we* are this tired, how do waitresses twice our age (I was in my early thirties at the time) do this, and how do they feel about their jobs? Are they bitter after years of dealing with difficult customers? Do they have dreams they never realized? Are they worn out from the physical and mental demands of the job? And what about those who worked in coffee shops? They average eight- to ten-hour shifts, and my workdays were only four to six hours. I made decent money serving sushi in a large, metropolitan city, but what about those who worked in greasy spoons in small, remote towns? What about health insurance? Aging in the workplace? Retirement?

The questions kept coming. So the following week I started asking people if they knew any older coffee shop waitresses. Many of them reenacted a stereotype of the wisecracking, gum-smacking diner waitress. I heard a story about a waitress in New Jersey who had a heavy East Coast accent and served customers with a cigarette hanging out of her mouth, looking discontented and disinterested. I heard another story about a lifer who wore teal-blue eye shadow and a towering red beehive. Although I was completely taken in by these colorful portraits, I had to wonder if these women really existed or if they were exaggerations triggered by Hollywood stereotypes. My mind was flooded with images of waitresses from films and television over the last seventy years—Bette Davis's tawdry, low-class hasher in *Of Human Bondage* (1934), Joan Crawford's wise and efficient waitress in *Mildred Pierce* (1945), the defiant "no substitutions" waitress who serves Jack Nicholson in *Five Easy Pieces* (1970), the trailer-park waitress played by Lily Tomlin in Robert Altman's *Short Cuts* (1993), and Ellen Burstyn in Martin Scorsese's *Alice Doesn't Live Here Anymore* (1974). This film inspired the hit television show

Alice, in which the sassy, foul-mouthed waitress Flo would scream, "Kiss my grits!" to her boss, Mel, and to her badly behaved customers. Suddenly my mission was not only to find real-life diner waitresses but also to flesh out the characters Hollywood had programmed into our heads.

I took my questions to the library (I was in graduate school at the time) and found that very little had been written about this subculture of aging coffee shop waitresses. Although there were several excellent books about waitressing—*Waitress: America's Unsung Heroine* by Elder and Rolens, *Dishing It Out: Waitresses and Their Unions in the Twentieth Century* by Dorothy Sue Cobble, *Nickel and Dimed: On (Not) Getting By in America* by Barbara Ehrenreich, *The Harvey Girls: Women Who Opened the West* by Lesley Poling-Kempes, *Hey, Waitress! The USA from the Other Side of the Tray* by Alison Owings, and *Dishing It Out: Power and Resistance among Waitresses in a New Jersey Restaurant* by Greta Foff Paules—only a few of these books addressed the older career waitresses who refer to themselves as "lifers," and none of them focused primarily on this group of aging workers. Realizing this window of opportunity, I decided to make them the subject of my thesis for my graduate degree in visual criticism at the California College of the Arts.

By the end of the month I was on the road with a digital camera, a mini-disc recorder, a scanner, and a map. To find the waitresses, I called the visitors' bureau and the chamber of commerce in the towns I planned to visit. I spoke to people who grew up in the area and inquired about their favorite local institutions. I called the restaurant, spoke with the manager, and asked if he or she could recommend the best waitresses who fit the parameters of the project. I did short telephone inquiries with the waitresses they recommended, sent out questionnaires, set up interview times, and asked them to gather old photographs and newspaper clippings that I could scan. I interviewed waitresses who lived in large cities and others who lived in rural, desert towns with only one stoplight. As a black woman, I was unsure how I would be received in some of these out-of-the-way places, but practically every location I visited offered the highest standards of hospitality. Small Town USA opened up their homes, uncovered their histories, and shared their lives with me. I left each town with more than just data for the project; the experience restored my belief in the kindness of strangers.

I have interviewed fifty-nine waitresses in forty-three cities. Each interview lasted one to three hours, all of which were transcribed, logged, and indexed for the book. Most of the waitresses are fifty years and older and have worked in coffee shops for at least twenty years. Although the technical definition of a diner is a prefabricated structure that is built in a factory and moved to a permanent location, usually somewhere in the northeastern United States, the terms "diner" and "coffee shop" are used interchangeably throughout the book to denote any casual restaurant.

Although many of the restaurants profiled in this book hadn't changed in years, I was careful not to be seduced by the trappings of nostalgia. Most of the places had been in operation since the 1950s, and as much as I was tempted to conjure up a rose-tinted past of virgins in bobby socks and poodle skirts, microwaves, computers, televisions, American flags, and "Support Our Troops" signs always brought me back to the present.

The criteria for the project was that the waitresses must work in a coffee shop (ideally a place that serves breakfast and has a counter with stools) that had become a staple in the community with a clientele of regular customers. Whether I was in a busy downtown San Francisco restaurant or a 150-year-old lunch counter in Glasgow, Kentucky, I saw waitresses participate in the daily ritual of people's lives. These eateries all had an element of sameness that the customers relied on. They liked the fact that the place hadn't changed in fifty years. The stools were covered in the same tattered vinyl that was worn soft from decades of use; the pattern on the Formica countertops was worn away in all the right places; the food was the same; and the waitresses had been there for as long as they could remember.

Having waitressed for almost a decade helped my research tremendously. I wasn't an outsider trying to understand the plight of the hard-working waitress. Instead, I was one of them. I had also spent many nights rubbing my swollen feet and I knew how painful it was to be yelled at by a hostile customer. They trusted me be-

BOULEVARD DINER, WORCESTER, MASSACHUSETTS

cause I spoke restaurant slang and we traded insider stories about the industry. Based on my own waitressing experience, I expected to meet women who felt overworked and underappreciated, but that's not what I found. All but a few said they loved their jobs and if given the opportunity, they "wouldn't do anything else." I thought, how can this be true? Waitressing can be a grueling, thankless job. And where were all the complaints about carpal tunnel and varicose veins?

After five more years of research and listening to heartfelt testimonies about the job, I took a closer look at their lives. I analyzed their work environment. I studied theorists, academics, and historians who wrote about sociology, gender, ethnography, labor, restaurants, spatial politics, and power. I read Michel Foucault, John Berger, Barbara Ehrenreich, James Clifford, Dorothy Sue Cobble, William Foote Whyte, Studs Terkel, Richard Gutman, Mike Rose, Victor Burgin, and many others. I considered that, although we had the same job, an older waitress's experience might be different from mine because we were raised in a different time. There were benefits to working in a casual environment, and career waitresses knew the tricks of the trade to make the job easier. In many cases, their seniority status earned them a higher hourly wage and respect from their coworkers and managers. Ironically, the physical and mental exercise kept them healthy instead of wearing them down, and most important, their regular customers made the job more enjoyable and profitable—they left better tips than strangers who were just passing through. Most of the career waitresses I interviewed were financially stable homeowners, drove newer cars, and many had sent their children to private schools.

This book is not a scholarly study, a memoir, or a historical account of waitressing. And even though there are photographs throughout the book, it's more than a coffee-table book of a pop culture icon. It combines interview excerpts, cultural criticism, photography, and oral history to recognize an overlooked group of working women who have brought meaning and culture to the American roadside dining experience. Each chapter takes a critical look at how career waitresses have taken a job that many people avoid and made it their livelihood. Although several waitresses are quoted throughout the book, their stories are featured at the end of the chapters. One chapter provides a brief history of diner culture and shows how women started working in diners. The book also demonstrates how career waitresses are different from average service workers; it investigates issues of power in the workplace, shows how older waitresses are physically able to handle the job, explains why they are sometimes disrespected, examines the

work ethic of their successors, and reveals why they choose to keep working well into their eighties.

Career waitresses do more than just serve food. They are part psychiatrist, part grandmother, part friend, and they serve every walk of American life: from the retired and the widowed, to the wounded and the lonely, and from the working class to the wealthy. Even though the classic diner waitress is an icon of American culture, it seems as though every month I hear about another mom-and-pop restaurant closing, and every year I get a letter from a waitress telling me that she retired or was being laid off. This book takes a moment to honor and recognize their contribution to our communities while they're still around because there is no guarantee who will replace them after they're gone. We have rightfully conditioned our youth to strive for "professional" jobs, but those who do end up waitressing their entire lives may feel differently about the job than this group of waitresses does.

It would be fair to say that these last seven years of doing this project has helped me to redefine my perspective on life, work, and happiness. It has made me reevaluate the myth of the American dream that says you need to have an "important" job to be happy. Suddenly, it made sense why some of those who finally achieve success, as determined by our culture, are on antidepressants trying to figure out why they're miserable. This is not to say that everyone should wait tables or get a regular job as an antidote to depression, but somewhere along the line in our quest for a "better" life, many of us forget what's really important: our health, our families, and our compassion to humanity. I now understand that fulfillment is not found in a 401k, a five-thousand-square-foot house, or an inflated job title. Most important, I learned that life is what you make it. So the next time you see a sixty-something-year-old waitress wiping down a table in a diner, don't feel sorry for her. More likely than not, she's content right where she is. Take it from Ruthie, a sixty-four-year old waitress in Sparks, Nevada, who says, "I just wish I had another thirty-five years to do it all over again."

Ketchup in Her Veins

Career waitresses are rare. In *Waitress: America's Unsung Heroines* Leon Elder and Lin Rolens write that one in five women has waitressed at some time in their lives, but only one in a hundred has what it takes to stay with the job. They walk, schlep, reach, lift, write, pour, clear, walk, wipe, socialize, prioritize, bend over, pick up, memorize tedious details, argue with the cook, and then walk some more. For the average worker, waitressing can be tough, but the career waitresses in this book are not average; they are a resilient group of hardworking women who have made an art out of waitressing. Not all career waitresses do the job well, nor are they saints, but in my experience the majority of them are professional caretakers and provide companionship to their community. They don't perceive themselves as servants, and they have risen above the bitter, cranky complainers who are waiting for a "real" job to come along. Lifers take waitressing seriously. They care if your bacon is soggy or if your hash browns are overcooked. They care if you're unhappy with your meal, because they understand how hard it is to eat when you're angry. They warm the coffee cup for their special customers; they make sure there is a fresh pot of decaf, because they know it can be the first pot to get stale. For their diabetic customers, they remember to bring sugar-free syrup. They know if your kid just graduated from college or spent the night in jail. They know if your car is in the shop and the test results of your last medical checkup. They share intimate stories about their lives and remember to ask about ailing family members. Their patience and love of people is genuine; it's not something they can fake for tips, because saccharine sentiment is often transparent. They can almost always find a warm spot in their heart for strangers. It's innate. Average, everyday servers aren't in the same league as the waitresses in this book. These women are the cream of the crop.

Most of the career waitresses I interviewed started working in restaurants in their early teens. Charlotte Solberg from Seligman, Arizona, remembered, "I was 13 when I started. My ex-brother-in-law, Bobby, broke me in. I was really shy, I didn't want to be around all those railroad guys; they were kind of rough. I would make mistakes. Sometimes, I would give them coffee with a soup spoon and they'd all laugh at me. It was a horseshoe counter and they all watched me. I would get so embarrassed. They'd tease me and say, 'I really like this glossy furniture.' I was so naïve. I asked Bobby what they meant and he said, 'They like you working here, because you're young.'"

Starting at an early age gave waitresses a leg up in the business. Those who were fortunate enough to work with older waitresses learned almost everything they needed to know just by watching.

JO ANN ARCHER, CRYSTAL DINER, LAWRENCEVILLE, NEW JERSEY

Virginia Brandon from Henderson, Nevada, said, "I was about fourteen when I started. The main waitress there was named Louise. She was probably only fifty years old, but she seemed really old to me. Her hair was cut like a man's, the way mine is today, and she only had one arm. I thought 'If she can do it with one arm, then I ought to be able to do it with two.'"

It takes time and practice to learn the skill of waitressing. Most servers can get the food to the table, but few perform as well as these lifers. The ones who are not cut out for the job struggle with the basics. "It's not natural for them," Susan Thurmond noticed after training waitresses at the Rainbow in Henderson, Nevada. The simple act of making toast told Susan practically everything she needed to know about whether a newcomer was going to last. "You don't put the toast in the toaster and stand there and wait until the toast is done and butter it. You can, but now you've got four new downs [tables] and you're way behind. You start your toast, walk away, and do something else." The few trainees who realized they were wasting precious time were naturals. But those who stood there hovering over the toaster never did the job well. After seeing waitresses come and go over the decades Susan would tell the laggers, "Waitressing is just not for you. It's not a bad thing; it's just not your thing."

Getting orders to the table appears to be a simple task, which is why waitressing is often thought of as an unskilled job. But newcomers quickly realize that there's a lot you have to know. Georgina Moore from Reno, Nevada, said, "People think we're are a dime a dozen, they think that anybody can do this job, but it's not true." The fact that most women serve their families at home every day may lead people to think that waitressing doesn't require skill. But serving a family of four is very different from waiting on thirty people during the lunch rush when everybody wants to order, eat, and leave in twenty minutes.

Waitressing isn't easy, and yet it is one of the most common jobs in America. According to the National Restaurant Association, over thirteen million people work in the industry, making it the largest employer in the United States outside of the government. People wait tables for the quick money that can be made, the flexibility of the work schedules, and the fact that it requires no formal education or experience. Most servers today are doing the job temporarily until a better one comes along. Jean Joseph of San Francisco, who has waitressed for over sixty years, thinks it's wrong to use waitressing as a means to an end. "It's a disgrace," she said with pursed lips. "Seventy percent of all waiters and waitresses out there should not be doing this."

To do the job well, waitresses have to effectively manage their space, time, money, and people. They must be quick, highly organized, focused, and self-sufficient multitaskers with a memory that rarely fails them. Because the job requires a genuine love of people, waitresses need an engaging personality and an uncanny intuition about the public. Despite the troublemakers, the cheapskates, and the prima donnas, they can deal with anyone who shuffles through the door. Most career waitresses say that their customers are the number one reason they continue to waitress. With brightness in her eyes Jean said, "When people walk through the door, something inside me changes and I just adore them. I really do."

Most people aren't psychologically or even physically equipped to handle a life of waiting tables. It takes a steady temperament, an uncompromising work ethic, and a strong physical constitution to be a lifer. Most waitresses said that, in retrospect, they didn't find the work to be physically difficult. The reason for this might be that more than half of the women interviewed grew up working on farms, picking cotton, tobacco, onions, and wheat. Those who didn't grow up doing farm work were raised from hearty stock and said that from an early age, physical labor was a daily part of their routine. They thought waitressing was easy compared to what they had been used to, and since they were active people, being confined to an office was not an option. They preferred having a flexible schedule so they could spend more time with their children. They also enjoyed the unpredictable environment of the restaurant industry and the fact that every workday promised to be different. After weighing all the pros and cons, for them, waitressing was a logical career choice. Virginia said, "I just can't imagine doing any other kind of work; this is my therapy. It's fun. I go to work to have fun."

Some career waitresses say they didn't love the job in the beginning, but after a while it grew on them and they didn't want to leave. After realizing they were going to waitress their entire lives, however, some had to look at the job differently and change their attitude. Still, most of them gushed over how much they enjoyed the job. Shirley Reed, a retired Los Angeles waitress, remembered, "It was like going to a party every night. I'd get all dressed up in my little white uniform. I absolutely loved it."

Was this simply nostalgia? When people reminisce, they often choose to remember the good times. After the first year of interviews, I thought surely it was a fluke that I had found over twenty career waitresses who happen to love their jobs. The portrait the media portrays of the aging diner waitress is a woman with a dismal life, hustling for coins and serving a demanding public that doesn't appreciate her efforts. Why weren't these women *exhausted*? After giving them every opportunity to talk with me, a former waitress, about the obvious disadvantages of the job, the majority still insisted, "If given the opportunity, I wouldn't do anything else" and "There's a lot more good to waitressing than bad." Rachel Lelchuk, who worked at Louis' Restaurant in San Francisco for fifty-five years and never took a formal vacation, said, "I made an art out of it. I took it seriously. For me, it was a holiday to come to work, because I looked forward to it."

JEAN JOSEPH, AL'S GOOD FOOD CAFE, SAN FRANCISCO, CALIFORNIA

COUNTER CULTURE

A seasoned waitress has a large, local following and is often the main attraction. Customers will wait for hours to sit with her, even if there are empty tables in other sections of the restaurant. Her regulars will call ahead to make sure she's working that day; others will wait outside and peer through the window to see if she's there. If a waitress quits and moves to another coffee shop, it's not unusual for her customers to follow her throughout her entire career.

With her freshly made hairdo and vibrant personality, Laverne Phillips has so much charisma she can turn a first-time customer into a faithful regular. While I was photographing Laverne at the Buena Vista Cafe, a San Francisco restaurant where she worked in the 1950s, a tourist visiting from Florida sitting at the bar remembered her from over twenty years earlier when she had waited on him at the Seven Seas Restaurant in Sausalito, a small bayside town outside of San Francisco. Although she had waited on him only once, he recognized her two decades later in a different city. When I asked him how he remembered Laverne, he simply said, "Well, how can you forget her?"

Rachel has received numerous awards for being a stellar waitress. She has been honored on several radio stations and has been written about in books and magazines in the United States, Europe, and Japan. When NPR's *Weekend America* played Rachel's story, people called in from all over the country asking about her. One of her customers from Glendale, California, wrote an email saying, "All it took was the sound of her voice to conjure a vision of her busy, bustling self dressed in a yellow-and-black horizontal-striped top that added to the impression of her as a busy bee. She was one of my all-time favorite waitresses. Rarely have I ever encountered a waitress with such enthusiasm for her job. It was a joy to be served by her."

JEAN JOSEPH, AL'S GOOD FOOD CAFE, SAN FRANCISCO, CALIFORNIA

Jean Joseph

Al's Good Food Cafe | San Francisco, California

I was born to waitress. I grew up in Flint, Michigan, and there were not too many choices for me. In school, I hated sitting at a desk, so I knew I was either going to end up working in a factory or on an assembly line and get married or I was going to be a waitress and make money. I've been waitressing for over sixty years. I started in 1947. My father won a restaurant in a card game. It was Ken's Cafe on North Saginaw Street in Flint, Michigan. I was working for this man, Ken, at the time. I walked in the next day and my father was my boss. He taught me to be a good waitress. We used to cut our potatoes by hand and we washed our own dishes. We would have our boyfriends come in to help peel potatoes and wash dishes. Back then they called it "pearl diving."

I love waitressing. I never had a desire to do anything else. I've always said that unless you love people, you shouldn't do this job. Just like an actress; it's something you're born with. You go into these places today where the wait staff don't care. It's terrible. I want someone to walk up to me and care that I am spending my dollar. I want people to treat me the way I would treat them. Instead, they write down your order and then they want you to leave them money. It's wrong.

I worked at the old Woolworth's restaurant in San Francisco and I worked for Greeks. When you work for Greeks, you're a good waitress, because they really train you. Today my family has thirteen restaurants. Most of them are in the San Francisco Bay area. We've been here on Mission Street at Al's since the 1970s. Everything is fresh. Everything is made from scratch. And you couldn't find more pleasant people than the ones who come in here. In fifteen or twenty years, you'll never find another restaurant like this. Never.

LINDA EXELER, COLONIAL COTTAGE, ERLANGER, KENTUCKY

Linda Exeler

Colonial Cottage | Erlanger, Kentucky

I've waited tables for thirty-eight years. In the entire time I've wait-ressed, I've worked at only two restaurants. We are all friends here at the Cottage. It's family. I grew up with some of the girls who work here. I've had some really trying times . . . some tragedies. I lost my dad and my mom and my brother . . . all in like eight months. But coming here helped me to get through it. And also, my customers gave me flowers and cards and then they'd give me big hug. It's like a bloodline here. When they hire new people, I know immediately, by their first day, if they're going to stay. Just by their attitude, if they say, "I'm just here to make my money . . ." they won't last.

When I started waiting tables, it was the best thing I ever did. I thought I'd better do something I'm going to enjoy. People say every time they come in here, I have the same attitude and the same personality. It's because I enjoy being here. And it is hard sometimes, because we do have some crazy customers. You'll get a customer that you couldn't please if you stood on your head. But before they leave, they're usually feeling better. In any case, I don't let them bring me down, just because they're having a bad day. When I was nine years old, my momma got real sick, and I had to take care of my brothers and sisters. So waitressing just came naturally, I guess.

Waitressing is my life. It's my calling. This is what I was born to do. I feel like God gave me a gift and this is what it turned out to be. I just feel I've been a very blessed person to have the ability to have feelings for people. I just have that kind of personality and strength to put up with what waitresses have to deal with.

I have some customers I've waited on for almost forty years. I've waited on four generations of the same family. I know everything they eat and drink. If the weather's bad, we call them on the phone, hoping that they don't come out and risk an accident—especially

the older people. A lot of them worked down at the barrel factory and I served them when I worked at the other restaurant. After I started working at the Cottage, they started coming in here. I waited on one gentleman from the age of 75 until he was 104 years old and then he finally passed, but I gave him his hundredth birthday cake. It was too cool.

We are really busy in here. I work the tea room by myself. I do that from six thirty in the morning until eleven. It seats forty-eight people. Plus on Wednesdays and Thursdays, I do the banquet room, with twenty-five people. I serve all of them breakfast and I know what every single one of them eats. It's upstairs so it's a hustle. If I get too busy, I stand in the middle of the room and I let them know what's going on. I tell them, "We'll get through this guys." They say, "Lynn, take your time. It's no problem." I've got some of 'em trained. They'll get up and get the coffee pot and serve it for me. And some even clean my tables [laughing], I swear to God. It's a riot. But I love the challenge and I enjoy the competition. If you see me in action, you'll see, I'm the best.

Rachel Lelchuk

Louis' Restaurant | San Francisco, California

I was born in Harbin, Manchuria, China. My mother and father came from Russia. I came to the United States, and I started working at Louis' in 1947. I worked there for fifty-five years. Louis' Restaurant is loved by thousands of people because it's friendly and respectful, the coffee is excellent, the food is delicious—it's quality. Today, it's different. In some restaurants, everything is kind of automatic. You have to ask for every little thing and you even feel embarrassed to do it, but at Louis' Restaurant, we have a very efficient attitude, we care.

Waitressing is my world. It was the most important thing in my life. I don't just wait on people, I want them to feel pleasantly, make sure everything is hot. I pick up their orders right away, their coffee should be nice and hot and tasty. I made an art out it.

Ninety-nine percent of my customers were unbelievably beautiful, and some became my friends. When I go to Borders Books or Safeway and see my customers, they say, "She never wrote down

I'm not college-educated, but I am self-taught because I do a lot of reading. I like art, classical music, opera, and the ballet. With my tips, I could afford to go to the opera and the ballet and buy beautiful books.

Mentally I'm the same as I was. I got a debilitating case of asthma and I had to quit waitressing at eighty-two. I think I may have gotten it from breathing in all the second-hand smoke over the years at Louis'. But I still miss the place. It's on my mind day and night [crying]. And my customers wrote me lovely letters, sent me beautiful flowers, and are still faithful.

RACHEL IN FRONT OF HER FIFTY-YEAR PLACARD AT LOUIS' RESTAURANT

our orders, she just remembered." I was at the opera last Friday night, and I met a customer there who I hadn't seen in twenty years and he remembered my name. Isn't that some small world? A year ago on my birthday, somebody at work got a book and all the customers wrote their comments in there. My customers have come from all over the world: Italy, France, England, Japan, Hong Kong, and they always wanted to take their picture with me and they would mail them to me and I value that very much.

Counter Intelligence

Diners were born in the late nineteenth century in New England. Horse-drawn lunch wagons were strategically stationed across from factories to serve workers simple food at reasonable prices. In those days, diners were purely a functional enterprise and comfort was not a priority. There was no place to sit, and all food transactions were conducted through a window. Men ate standing up outside in snow, rain, fog, and hail. Eventually the extreme weather conditions pressured diner manufacturers to create an interior space so patrons could have shelter.

Until the 1920s, men dominated the diner industry (including the wait staff). Consequently, many women of that time had never even seen the inside of a diner. Like most enterprising businessmen, diner operators wanted to increase their sales during the hours when most of their clientele was at work. They soon realized that women were a large, untapped market. In an attempt to attract the fairer sex, diners served salads and set out props such as baby carriages, shrubs, and flower boxes with signs announcing "Ladies Invited." Still, women avoided diners. The small, backless stools that lined the counter were extremely uncomfortable and unlady-like. To address the problem, manufacturers designed diners with tables and booths. When diners succeeded at attracting women, male patrons complained about having to watch their language and their manners, stirring up a hot debate among diner operators. In 1927, *Dining Car News* featured the controversy. Waiters grumbled that women ate too slowly and took too long to order. An article published at the time in *Dining Car News*, "Do Women Take Longer to Eat Than Men Do?" revealed that there was no difference in eating times between the sexes; each took an average of ten to thirteen minutes. Still, men didn't like women moving in on their territory. Some diners resolved the issue by segregating the space by gender. The Flying Yankee dining car in Pennsylvania, for example, sat women only in the basement.

During World War II, companies lost their manpower to the war, and women were suddenly asked to perform jobs they had previously been excluded from. They were recruited to do everything from construction work to welding war equipment. Diners were no different. It wasn't long before operators recognized the benefits of having waitresses. They thought women were more responsible, and more importantly, they could pay them almost half the wages and yield twice the amount of work. In a 1941 article in *The Diner* magazine, Sam Yellin listed the advantages of having women work in diners:

1. Women will work for less pay.
2. Women won't stay out late drinking and call in sick the next day.
3. Women belong around food.
4. Women will work harder than men.
5. Women are always happy.
6. Women are more efficient workers.
7. Women are more honest than men—they don't steal.
8. Women can talk and work at the same time.
9. Women clean diners better than men.
10. Women are cleaner than men.
11. The customers like women better.
12. Customers don't swear in front of women.

From then on, waitresses became fixtures in the diner, but not in the way owners had intended. They assumed that women would be docile, kind, and obedient. While there were those who fit that stereotype, others found independence and financial stability through waitressing. Then came the 1960s and a shift in female empowerment. It was a time when women's work was being analyzed in the media, Aretha Franklin reminded women to demand respect, Betty Friedan's seminal book, *The Feminine Mystique*, was a best seller, Eleanor Roosevelt led the President's Commission on the Status of Women, and the National Organization for Women (NOW) was created. This second wave of feminism surely trickled down into the restaurant industry and inspired waitresses to lay

VINTAGE PHOTOGRAPH OF WAITRESSES AT THE BUTTER CREAM BAKERY & DINER.
COURTESY OF THE BUTTER CREAM BAKERY & DINER.

down new ground rules about how much nonsense they would take. Though a waitress may not have owned the diner, when she worked the counter it became her territory. She had the authority to throw out problem customers and people relied on her to keep the place under control.

Counters: The Power of Convenience

The counter is an incredibly convenient workspace designed for speed and efficiency. It's located in front of the kitchen window, so the waitress can grab the food, walk a few steps, and set it down right in front of the customer. At the counter, her movements are more precise and she is able to observe a larger area. If she were table serving, she would have to walk across the restaurant while carrying multiple plates of food.

For easier service, some older diners have mirrors on the ceiling above the counter so the waitress can quickly check for coffee refills and empty plates by simply glancing upward. (With table serving she has to walk the entire length of the restaurant to check for refills). At the counter she has everything she needs right at her fingertips. The coffee, soups, condiments, shakes, desserts, and kitchen window are only a few steps away. Counters are waist high, allowing her to serve with minimal bending, leaning, or reaching. A booth, on the other hand, is much lower; not only does she have to walk across the restaurant to get to it, but she also has to balance the plates while bending and reaching to serve the food.

At the counter, regulars congregate, tip, and leave. The constant turnover of this section gives the waitress a clear advantage over serving tables and booths where people camp out and sometimes

REGULAR AT THE BEL AIRE DINER, PEABODY, MASSACHUSETTS

stay for hours. Also, the stools position the customer higher, facing the waitress. More opportunity for eye contact strengthens her connection. And since many regulars come in alone, they don't get lost in conversation with companions and tend to talk to their waitress instead. Counter customers also respect and understand more about a waitress's job because they are sitting in front of her workstation and can see her working. If they are waiting for something they feel confident that she hasn't forgotten about them because they are sitting right in front of her. Mike Ghirabaldi goes to the

Butter Cream Bakery & Diner in Napa two to three times a week: "When I sit at the counter, I watch Sondra. She'll have ten orders up and ten different things going at once. . . . She's running back and forth. I've even seen her cook orders when the cook is on break. It's amazing."

There are both physical and psychological consequences for waitresses who are stuck serving in inefficient stations. A table server will walk what appear to be only a few extra steps per trip to her tables. But after an eight-hour shift, she has literally walked a few more miles than the counter waitress, and during those extra miles she's balanced heavy plates and carried hundreds of drinks, increasing the opportunity for accidents. High maintenance customers who send her back and forth to the kitchen take a toll. A common complaint among table servers is when they ask a large table of customers about drink refills and only one person answers yes. After walking across the restaurant to order the drink or to make it herself at the drink station, walking back to the table, and setting it down, someone else will pipe up, "Oh, could I have a refill?" The waitress goes back, performs the same tasks, and returns to the table only to be sent away yet again for another drink refill. It's no wonder that counter waitresses feel more efficient. The psychological satisfaction of getting so much done with half the effort gives her confidence and makes her job much easier.

Practically every item found in a diner is designed to be functional for the customer and to make a waitress's job easier and

safe. In the Bauhaus tradition, diners are the perfect example of form follows function. Seasoning shakers, metal napkin holders, and plastic squeeze bottles are loaded with utilitarian sensibility and elegance. They are iconic in their simplicity. Take, for instance, a sugar shaker's glass belly that is designed to fit perfectly in our hands. All condiment holders are completely smooth with no ridges or edges that will gather dirt and grime, making it easier for the waitress to clean. Although chrome-edged Formica tables are aesthetically pleasing, their primary purpose is practicality. Formica, a heat-resistant material invented in 1913, was a staple as a countertop laminate in diners by the 1940s. It was more durable and less expensive than the metal, wood, and porcelain enamel that had been used previously in diners. Tables and chairs curve at the corners to avoid injury and are easier for the waitress to maintain and clean. Metal appliances, equipment, and backsplashes inhibit bacteria growth, and the stylized patterns printed on Formica mask syrup and coffee drips until the waitress can steal a minute to wipe down the counter while her customers are none the wiser.

Ironically, the space that women once avoided—the counter—proved to be the most lucrative. Serving more customers increases a waitress's tips by a large margin. Consequently, it can take years for a waitress to claim the counter as her primary workstation. Susan Thurmond of the Rainbow in Henderson, Nevada, said, "A lot of the newcomers can't handle the counter. It's just too fast for 'em." When Susan is "on counters" she's guaranteed a hundred customers on her day shift, compared to the back area (table service) where waitresses average only sixty. "Even on my day off," she said, "if there is a counter shift available, I'll work it."

Ordering Systems

Ordering systems in restaurants have changed considerably since the turn of the twentieth century. Fern Osborn, who waitressed at the Copper Cart on Route 66, said, "Back in the old days we used to 'call 'em in.'" It was standard for waitresses to shout diner lingo that only staff members or regular customers could understand, and calling in orders fit right in with the off-the-cuff camaraderie

that diner patrons came to know and love. A "grease spot" was a hamburger. If you wanted it with cheese it was a "CB." In some restaurants, especially on the East Coast, diners got creative with naming their orders. "Blonde and sweet" was coffee with cream and sugar, Jell-O was "nervous pudding," and "Adam and Eve on a raft" was two scrambled eggs on toast.

The challenge of calling in orders fell mostly on the cook, who not only had waitresses yelling at him all day but also had to memorize the orders for the entire restaurant. Louis' Restaurant in San Francisco operated like this since the 1930s. The owner, Tom Hontalas, who cooked for many years, said, "It was hard to remember the orders, but we liked it that way. Maybe it was an ego thing, to see if we could do it. But as the years passed it got more difficult to find cooks who could remember, so we switched to having the waitresses write down the orders."

Ellen Warren-Seaton, who manages the USA Country Diner in New Jersey, said, "A waitress isn't just an order-taker. She has to know how to tell the cook exactly what she needs. She can't just write '2 eggs over'—she has to tell the cook how many eggs she

LINDA EXELER,
COLONIAL COTTAGE,
ERLANGER, KENTUCKY

wants on how many plates. Diners have a universal ordering system. '1 on 1' is one egg on one plate, or a '2 on 1' is two eggs on one plate. . . . If she doesn't do this, the cook has no idea what she wants."

Management also found that writing down orders minimized arguments between the cooks and the waitresses. If an order came up that a waitress didn't recognize, there was a written record of what she had given to the cook, making it easier for everyone to move on and get back to work.

Switching to Computers

Career waitresses spend years cultivating and perfecting their ordering system. When a manager announces a switch to computers, lifers panic. Some beg, plead, and cry, while others threaten to quit. In an environment where time is so critical, it's a terrifying transition for waitresses who have been calling in orders or writing out their tickets for over thirty years. When the Colonial Cottage switched to using computers, Linda Exeler said, "It was pitiful. We were all crying. I didn't even want to come back to work. I just went home and prayed." But Linda eventually worked through her fear. "I got it together," she said, "and came in with an open mind. I practiced with the computer on my off hours. Now I can place twenty orders in five minutes."

Another advantage of using a computer is that it can add up the check in seconds. Without a computer, waitresses have to be fast with the calculator and accurate with prices and sales tax, which is an overwhelming task when everyone wants their check at the same

time. But computers have made it much easier; the waitress simply prints the check, and all the calculations are itemized instantly.

The Diner Preference

Peggy Sue's 50's Diner in the desert town of Yermo, California, has a sign above the door that reads: "We reserve the right to refuse service to anyone—Regardless of who you are, who you think you are, who your daddy is, or how much money you make." In diners, fur coats hang next to cowboy hats while Jaguars and junkers sit side by side in the parking lot. Diner patrons tend to be friendlier than customers in upscale restaurants, where they expect a different type of service. In fact, when people are spending more money, they often expect a servant. "I prefer working in diners," said Sammi DeAngelis, a waitress at the Seville Diner in New Jersey. "I've done the fine dining where people think that because the checks are high,

you're supposed to kiss their butt. People who spend $200 for dinner think that you owe them something. I don't care if the bill is $2 or $200, I treat everybody the same."

Most waitresses said they preferred working in a place with a large, regular clientele. When they worked at more upscale restaurants they missed the casual rapport with customers, and the staff always had to be ready to make a good first impression on strangers. But in a diner formalities are left at the door. In her Kentucky drawl, Mae Christmas said, "I could never work in a fancy restaurant. I'm too liable to holler at people and ask them if they want their usual when they come through the door. You can't do that in a fancy place." In diners, waitresses are also free to tell their customers exactly what they think about the latest political scandal or local gossip, whereas the staff in upscale restaurants is trained to keep conversation to a minimum and to never discuss religion, race, or politics.

Diner waitresses are rewarded for sharing their personality and their mood with the locals. Some days, waitresses are pleasant; other days they may be indifferent or even cranky. There's an authenticity and honesty in diners that is missing in our everyday lives. In a society obsessed with surface and image and a culture where chain stores mandate employees to speak to every customer who walks through the door, it's refreshing to come to a mom-and-pop diner where people know each other and the staff can be themselves. Mae said, "I really think the day of the mom-and-pop restaurants are just about over. The older generation is dying out and it's hard for the newer generation to understand this." Even though there are regulars who sit and socialize at the counter at chain restaurants, corporate rules are still in effect. To avoid lawsuits, the staff monitors what they say to each other and to their customers, making it a more structured, formalized, and regulated place. Mae is right: it is a different world.

MAE CHRISTMAS, EDITH'S CAFE, CENTRAL CITY, KENTUCKY

MAE CHRISTMAS, EDITH'S CAFE, CENTRAL CITY, KENTUCKY

Mae Christmas

Edith's Cafe | Central City, Kentucky

I grew up here in Central City, Kentucky, also known as the "capital of coal mining." My dad was a coal miner. My brothers worked in the mines too. When they closed the mines down, it was hard on everybody. There's not a lot of jobs around here, so I don't think I'd make more money doing anything else. With waitressing, the money's pretty good. It's usually more than if I got a job in a factory. A lot of people might not understand that.

Central City is just a small hometown, everybody knows everybody. Especially if you're a waitress, you're going to know just about everybody in town. If you're busy, customers will help clean tables because it's just like home to them. A lot of our customers order the same thing everyday, so we don't need to write down the orders, the cook knows, so we just write the customer's name down on the ticket. But you've got to remember who gets what, because it's terrible when you take the wrong food to the wrong table and these other people have been waiting ten minutes and there's their food at the wrong table and somebody else is eating it.

I've been waitressing for forty-two years. It's not easy work but I do enjoy it. At Edith's I do everything. I bus the tables, wait on the people, get the register. . . . You get tired because you make a lot of steps in a restaurant, back and forth, back and forth, you know. And sometimes in here, we might not get a break, period. So yeah, I'm pretty tired when I go home, but when I'm off a day or two, I'm ready to hit it again. In the last fourteen years I've haven't taken more than a week off for vacation.

One day we were really, really busy, I mean just packed. All the tables was dirty so I had a full bus tub and I sat it on the end of a chair. The chair fell and all the dishes went all over the floor and it just made the awfulest mess you ever seen and I was too busy to clean it up. I guess that was probably the worst day.

I never had any desire to work in a fancy restaurant. Here, it's just a more friendly atmosphere. I can holler at my customers and joke around. Most of my regulars come in and say, "I knew you were here Mae, I could hear you laughing outside."

REGULAR CUSTOMERS AT EDITH'S CAFE, CENTRAL CITY, KENTUCKY

ELLEN WARREN-SEATON, USA COUNTRY DINER, WINDSOR, NEW JERSEY

Ellen Warren-Seaton

USA Country Diner | Windsor, New Jersey

I started waitressing when I was fourteen. I worked as a car hop in Yakima, Washington. We wore white pedal pushers and white tops and on my first day I wore a strawberry shake down the front of me.

When I came out east in 1960, I must have worked in almost every diner in Staten Island. I also worked the Jewish delis. It was tough because the New York diners had different terminologies. We used a lot of slang to place orders: 81, 82, 83 means that's how many glasses of water you need. 81 is one glass, 82 is two glasses, etc. . . . A "whiskey down" was rye toast and "burn a hay" was a strawberry shake. Out west if you asked for "black and white" it meant you got a black-and-white ice cream soda, but here it's different. We didn't have egg creams in Washington either, so adjusting to the terminology here on the east coast was one of the biggest challenges of my waitressing career.

I did other kinds of work, but I always came back to waitressing. I was in banking for over thirty years. I've worked in bigger restau-

rants, but I never cared for 'em. I stayed with the diner because diners had better hours that worked with raising my kids. I worked on Wall Street from nine to five so when I got off work. I was able to go in for a six o'clock shift and work 6 pm to 6 am in the morning on the weekends.

This restaurant is probably sixty years old. It started out as a drive-in hot dog stand. We have a nice family of steady customers. A lot of people find us here when they get off the turnpike on their way down south. We get people from New York, Staten Island, Pennsylvania . . . all over. And they come back year after year. The first time they come, if they liked the food and if you make an impression on them, they'll be back to see you. It may be a whole year, but they'll be back. We also have a lot of customers who grew up in this area that have moved away and when they come home to see their families this is where they come, because it reminds them of their childhood. It means so much to them that we're still here.

SAMMI DEANGELIS, SEVILLE DINER, EAST BRUNSWICK, NEW JERSEY

Sammi DeAngelis

Seville Diner | East Brunswick, New Jersey

Waitressing is 90 percent personality and 10 percent performance. I'm almost always in a good mood, when people ask me, "Hi, how are you?" I say, "I'm terrific." I'm never good. I'm always terrific. I had someone say to me, "How come you never have a bad day?" I said, "Well, I'm not on fire and I have a healthy daughter. Everything else I encounter, I can either fix or I can't fix."

I started waitressing right out of high school. When I was eighteen, I had a bad experience that should have killed it for me. I was carrying four or five platters of hot turkey, mashed potatoes with extra gravy when a three-year-old boy cut me off. It was either dump it on him or me. I had no choice so I dumped it on me. That was the time of the nylon uniforms, and the uniform stuck to me like wallpaper paste. My boss Margie basically stripped me right on the floor with everybody standing there. I had on a half-slip and bra and she just pulled my uniform right off and grabbed a cold wet towel and threw it on the front of me, which is the reason I have no scars. Thank God for her. I went to the hospital with second-degree burns. After that, there was a sign posted in the restaurant: Children Shall Remain Seated.

I grew up in this business and my dad taught me that everyone is treated like family. If you won't eat it yourself or if you wouldn't serve it to your family, you *don't* bring it out of the kitchen. So that's the way I do things. If I ordered it rare, I want it rare, I don't want it medium-rare. Within a couple of minutes, I want it on the table. I want you eating it. I want you happy.

I like diner work better than fine dining. I'm trained in fine dining so I can make the pink scrolls. I can serve a $1,500 dollar bottle of champagne and never make a faux pas. I know proper service: I don't like it. I get tipped pretty well, not perfectly, but pretty well. I usually make out better than the other girls. I try to anticipate everyone's needs and I'm fast. I'm really fast. While the other girls are ringing $600 a night, I'm ringing $1,000. There are girls who work really hard and then there are the ones who don't give a darn about anything. They come in and make their money and they don't even care about their customers. That really upsets me. They're the people who are putting a roof over your head, you know. It's the difference between making $2 on a table and making $5. Don't be mad at me, because I go the extra mile for my customers. I take it seriously. As long as they can seat me, I can fly and do it. I'm here to turn my tables and get the food out, hot, fast and fresh. But I have fun with my customers. I tell them, "Sit down, eat your food, and don't bother me, and if you don't eat your food, you don't get dessert." And I walk away. It's a joke but Shakespeare said, "The truest word is oft times spoke in jest."

I was a body builder and a dancer up until about three years ago. When I was younger I did ballet, I was accepted at Juilliard. Now, I'm fifty-seven years old. You want to be gorgeous like I am? You gotta work at it, girlfriend. I kid around and say, "You think you can stay this gorgeous by sitting on your butt? No, gravity works, honey." That's why my butt's not that big, because I don't sit on it. You have to make the body work. With this job, carrying trays is like weight resistance training when you go to the gym. So I'm not only getting paid for this, I'm making tips and I'm staying in shape. Instead of walking, I can walk quickly because it's better for the heart. I have a bad spine and even though I have pain, I just keep going. I want to be ninety and still working.

Tricks of the Trade

Paul Montagna's book *Occupations and Society* lists waitressing among the "least skilled" jobs a woman can have, but most lifers say it takes about fifteen years to turn waitressing into an art. A newcomer's only formal training is offered from the manager in bite-size pieces that make things easier for the customer and for the restaurant but not for her. She learns table numbers, the menu, how to do her side work, where to drop off food orders, and how to do her paperwork at the end of the shift. She is not trained in the delicate balancing act of organizing her time, the customers, the cooks, and her workstation; and more important, she is not taught how to make tough, last-minute decisions when the place is packed with hungry laborers. Those skills come only with experience. But if she pays attention, lessons are passed down like orders that spin on the kitchen's ticket wheel. Jodell Kasmarsik of the Pie 'n Burger in Pasadena, California, who has been waitressing for over forty years, said, "You wanna learn how to do this? Then you've got to watch the older waitress because she knows. She's the pro."

Karesse Klein, a middle-aged waitress who has worked with Rachel DeCarlo, a seventy-seven-year-old server at Sittons North Hollywood Diner, said, "Rachel is never hectic. Everybody who works here, even the twenty-year-olds, reach a certain point when you get slammed [many customers at once] and you're running around with an idiotic expression on your face because you're so busy you can't even think straight. And then there's Rachel in the middle of it all—gliding—her customers get perfect service and they all love her. It's like watching Fred Astaire dancing. She makes it look effortless."

Veteran waitresses can show newer ones how to handle the lunch rush without breaking a sweat, but the job gets easier only after "doing her time" or, in essence, becoming a lifer. Two waitresses working the same shift can have entirely different experiences. Without skill, practice, and experience, younger waitresses *are* working harder than their senior counterparts. The primary difference is that inexperienced waitresses have fewer regular customers, so they are required to perform all the formal steps of service: She (1) greets the customer, (2) takes their order, (3) walks to the kitchen, (4) drops off the order, (5) walks to the drink station, (6) makes the drinks, (7) walks to the table, (8) serves the drinks, (9) walks back to the kitchen, (10) picks up the order, (11) walks to the table, (12) serves the food, (13) checks for drink refills, (14) walks back to the drink station, (15) refills the drinks, (16) returns to the table, (17) serves the drinks, (18) walks away from the table, (19) adds up the bill, and (20) finally walks back to the table to drop off the check. Multiply these twenty steps by at least six (because most

RACHEL DECARLO, SITTONS NORTH
HOLLYWOOD DINER, NORTH HOLLYWOOD,
CALIFORNIA

(RIGHT) BETTY MURPHY, MASTORIS DINER,
BORDENTOWN, NEW JERSEY

waitresses serve anywhere from 6 to 14 tables) and don't forget to include the extra trips for condiments, sauces, and special requests (which average about fifty trips around the restaurant per hour), and if she works an eight-hour shift, she's made about four hundred laps around the restaurant that day. The seasoned waitress who serves mostly regular customers, however, simply walks to the table and asks, "The usual?" They nod, and she walks away, reducing twenty serving steps to less than ten.

It's fair to say that an inexperienced waitress can handle the extra physical work, but even though her legs can walk the extra miles, she's often anxious or even preoccupied that she may have forgotten something. Experienced waitresses don't go through the same mental anxiety that novice waitresses do, recounting every step and going over the orders in their heads, which is why inexperienced waitresses don't carry the same air of confidence, nonchalance, or even as many plates as experienced waitresses do. After eight hours of circling the restaurant and hustling for tips from strangers, it's not surprising that newcomers are overwhelmed and exhausted by the job.

From the moment a skilled waitress approaches the table, there is never any doubt about her ability to do her job. An invisible boundary surrounds the table and the waitress has to claim ownership of that area. Control of this space puts the customer at ease and makes them feel secure and taken care of. Newer waitresses are often timid when they approach the table, afraid they will knock over a glass or nervous that they might be serving food that the customer didn't order. It's a moment of weakness. And most patrons can sniff it out immediately, leading to doubt, worry and fear that something will go wrong with their order. If something does go wrong, they can become immediately defensive, because their irritation and impatience has been brewing. Those initial moments at the table are critical and will set the tone for the entire meal. If the waitress doesn't prove herself in the beginning, she can rarely recover a customer's faith in her abilities. Some of the newer waitresses don't know how handle angry customers. One too many mean-spirited remarks or hateful stares can send her into

the kitchen in tears. When this happens to younger waitresses at the Rainbow in Henderson, Nevada, an experienced waitress like Susan Thurmond is sent over to deal with the problem customer. She said, "When I walk over to the table, I'm thinking 'Okay buddy, try and make me cry.' Or sometimes I'll make it into a game and I say to myself 'I will make you laugh before you leave here. Watch me.'"

Experienced waitresses can read their customers and tell immediately if someone requires extra face time or prefers to be left alone. Kathleen Woody, a waitress at Ryan's in Florence, Alabama, said, "Some customers give you a look that says, 'Give me my coffee, go away and be quiet.'" Knowing intimate details about the personality and habits of the restaurant staff helps. If a waitress knows her cook is nursing a hangover or going through a divorce, she may have more patience or stay out of his way to avoid a scene. Without critical insider information, her job can be like a minefield, never knowing who is going to explode and why. And when people do become mean, lifers must be thick skinned. Insults and arrogant demands bounce right off them. She accidentally spills coffee on a silk shirt? She knows what to say to calm down an irate customer. Someone throws a tantrum and makes her life miserable for a few minutes? She doesn't let it get to her. A green waitress may go into the kitchen and complain to everyone about what happened or go outside to smoke a cigarette to calm her nerves. She may even go into bathroom and cry, while her food orders pile up on the line. Soon, the incident has cost her so much time she is at the point where she can't catch up. Jodell said, "Us older waitresses don't sweat the small stuff." She knows they will be gone within the hour, so she moves on and focuses on her well-behaved patrons; she may even tell her regulars about it for a good laugh.

Being out of synch with her environment can make the job almost unbearable. All of her internal clues about how to make things run smoothly are off by seconds, causing a cascade of problems. Her appetizers come up at the same time as the entrees because the fry cook had a tantrum in the kitchen. Or every time she shows up to a table, her customers seem to want something ten

seconds after she leaves. And no matter what she does, she can't seem to please anybody—her flow and connection with people feels strained and unnatural. Things can go from bad to worse in seconds. Five minutes to a hungry ditch digger who doesn't trust his waitress can feel like forever. If the customer knows that she's on top of her game, he feels tended to, even if she's not there. Experienced waitresses develop this trust with their regulars, so even when she's having an off day, they will understand, and intuitively she knows this. But once a patron gets a whiff of doubt and starts tapping their foot and looking around to see where she is, it's all

downhill. On days like these, "Cheech" Kormos, a younger Los Angeles waitress at Ed Dabevic's, said, "I feel like I've been run over by a truck."

If waitresses fall behind, they can feel overwhelmed, confused, and hopeless. One by one, like dominoes, everything crumbles. It's called "getting in the weeds." The weeds sprout when she senses that her organization has slipped from her control, and although everything looks okay to the outsider, she's not sure if she placed the order for table 12's food, and then she remembers that table 16 didn't get their syrup heated like they asked. As the orders pile up, she can't remember what she was going to do next. Stress and anxiety have caused her to make so many mistakes that her customers have lost faith in her and shoot evil looks at her as she walks by. The cook is fed up with having to remake her orders because either she delivered them to the wrong table or didn't write them down correctly. Another term waitresses use when they are in the weeds is "buried," an accurate term for how it feels to have lost control of her section. If a waitress has too many days like this, it's likely she will quit and find another job.

Most lifers couldn't remember the last time they were in the weeds. It's all about maintenance and monitoring her environment. Career waitresses set up their stations with everything in reach, so they can walk the fewest steps possible. If a waitress sees her food is up for tables 3, 6, and 8 but table 7 was seated over five minutes ago and table 4 is waiting for a check, she delegates. She may ask her busser to water and coffee her new table and ask a fellow waitress to help run her food, which frees her up to take table 7's order and drop off table 4's check on the way.

GERI SPINELLI, MELROSE DINER, PHILADELPHIA, PENNSYLVANIA

The Case for Carrying

Carrying is her lifeline. The fewer trips she makes, the faster she can turn her tables; the faster she can turn her tables, the more money she earns. Experienced waitresses can carry four to six cups of coffee at a time. Geri Spinelli, who works at the Melrose Diner in Philadelphia, said, "It's easy. You just pile one cup on top of the other. But you have to work in a place that still uses saucers so that they fit together."

Veteran waitresses can carry up to seven plates on one arm, but this takes years—and a great deal of confidence—to master. If she's trained for arm service, it's very difficult for her to learn tray service and vice versa. Older waitresses prefer to carry with their arms. It's an old-fashioned technique that is not taught today in restaurants. Dolores Jeanpierre at Ole's Waffle Shop in Alameda, California, said, "We never used trays. I can carry a lot more on my arms. I tease the cooks and say, 'These legs are too old to be going back and forth.'"

Today servers are trained to carry plates on large trays, but most lifers will refuse to learn tray service. Fern Osborne of the Copper Cart in Seligman, Arizona, said that when a restaurant she worked for decided to start making the servers use trays, "Everybody threatened to quit. So they did away with that idea." If they are forced to learn tray service, many will try to carry the food at waist level, causing lower-back pain and possible injury. "It would kill my back," Edie Schrage remembered when she was learning. To carry large trays, they have to hoist the tray up over their shoulder, which can weigh up to forty pounds. Most career waitresses feel that carrying trays is too awkward and ends up being more work. They have to walk to get the tray and then get the stand to sit the tray on, forcing them to take extra steps and carry even more things to the table— not good for a waitress. Older waitresses also prefer arm service because the plates are carried at chest level and they can look down and see the food on the way to the table and make a mental note of who will be served first when they arrive. If they are carrying a tray, when they reach the table, they have to balance the tray from their shoulder, set it down on the stand, and then serve the food. The stands are often big and block the aisles. After the food is served, they have to put the tray and the stand away before they can do anything else. With arm service, once they serve the food, their hands are free to pick up dirty plates on their way back to the kitchen.

To carry multiple meals at a time, waitresses develop an inherent sense of balance and equilibrium. They don't balance equal weight on each side of their body as a gymnast would. Instead, waitresses excel at carrying uneven weight. Career waitresses can carry four loaded plates weighing up to twenty pounds on their left arm (if she's right handed), and only a couple of glasses weighing less than five pounds in their right hand. When placing the glasses down on the table, they almost never feel the need to turn around and check to see if the plates are about to fall, they don't even think about it.

Carrying so many plates over the decades has allowed their bodies to physically adapt to the job. Thick ceramic plates loaded with food can weigh up to seven pounds each. Often, they carry four or five plates at a time, three on the left arm and one or two with the right hand. Those extra twenty pounds pressing on the inside of their forearms not only build strong, powerful muscles but also flatten out the area like a makeshift tray, allowing them to achieve absolute control as they make a beeline to the table with all the food intact. Fern remembered, "It had to be perfect. You had your three plates, and to not break your egg yolk, you had to know how to stack your toast. When you went to the table and put everything down, it was in the right order. Your toast, then your jelly etc. . . . Those plates were so heavy! I used to go home and practice."

Waitresses use every finger and flat surface on their hands for carrying. Most people use their thumbs, index, and pinky fingers far more than their two middle fingers. Experienced diner waitresses, however, use their index and middle fingers more than the average person. Those fingers are needed to balance a lower plate while stacking another plate on the pinky, and thumb, creating a space between the plates so the upper plate almost levitates above the lower. Although this is a common carrying technique, not all waitresses master it. It takes years to build up the tiny muscles in

the middle fingers to tier plates so the food doesn't get smashed. The tendons from the middle fingers are attached to small bones in the wrists that connect to muscles that extend up to the elbow. Merely holding one's hand in this position is awkward and challenging; doing it while carrying ten to twenty pounds is a staggering feat that most waitresses never get credit for.

Brenda Hirst, a waitress at the Silver Spoon in Kingman, Arizona, hates it when waitresses let the bottom of the upper plate touch the food on the lower plate. "It's my pet peeve," she said. "If a waitress serves food like that to me, I tell her to take it back. I don't want my food touching the bottom of another plate. You don't know what's on the bottom of that plate."

Walking without bouncing is another skill that waitresses need to master. Pedometer readings show the average waitress logs eight to ten miles per shift. Stabilizing their upper body, loaded with food and drinks, while their legs tread for miles is a skill developed over time. Waitresses learn how to walk fast but never look like they're rushing. Confidence is critical. If a waitress is nervous about carrying, she'll not only walk slower but her anxiety will affect her balance. Like a well-trained acrobat on a tightrope who monitors every step, if she looks down, she will inevitably lose her balance and fall.

Memorizing Orders

Doing her best requires more from a waitress than just getting the food to the table. She also has to make sure she gets the order right. Georgina Moore from Reno, Nevada, said, "People think this job is easy, but I'd like to see them remember 'the usual' for two hundred people you wait on everyday. And then some regulars will say, 'Oh, I don't want my usual, I'll have what I had yesterday.' And then you have to stop and think and remember. But you just train yourself to do it."

Not only do waitresses have to remember to hold the mayo on some burgers and put extra pickle chips on others, they also manage to organize all the tedious details for about a hundred patrons per shift. Fern remembered, "Years ago waitresses didn't use trays or tickets; there was no 'wheel' to place orders on for the cook, you had to 'call 'em in.'" Fern is convinced that they made more mistakes when they switched to writing down orders. "It was all in here [points to her foot-high beehive]." Filed away with the customers' orders were also other distinguishing characteristics to help her anticipate any special needs. Today, with the computer, there are so many back-ups to help waitresses remember. Some lifers argue that this is why the quality of service is going downhill. If someone needs a drink refill and they forget what the customer is drinking, they just look at the ticket or check the computer, or even, God forbid, ask the customer. Some career waitresses would never do this; they consider that sloppy, second-rate service.

Burn and Turn

Virginia Brandon, age 68, works at the Rainbow coffee shop located inside a casino in Henderson, Nevada. At the Rainbow waitresses are trained to turn their tables as quickly as possible because upper management wants customers back out in the casino gambling.

Virginia said, "We're faster than McDonalds. They want servers who can 'burn and turn'" (work as fast as they can so the restaurant can seat consecutive customers). "A four-top [table with four people] can sit, order, eat and be the hell out of here in twenty minutes. You put your toast in the toaster, hang your check, and them eggs will be cooked before that toast pops up, and I'm not exaggerating. On my dinner shift, nobody takes a break. From five o'clock to nine o'clock you've got a waiting line of an hour, and so you don't have a cigarette, you don't go to the bathroom, you don't even breathe— you just run, yelling at everyone in your way, 'Behind ya! Behind ya! Coming through, arms loaded!' If you don't get out the way, you're gonna get knocked out."

To the casual observer, working at this pace seems brutal, but these women thrive in the madness. Jodell said with a serious look, "Sometimes the orders come up so fast, you can't keep up with them. You really have to hustle. But I love it. The busier it is, the better I like it."

The reward for managing chaos is the tip. Sprinting through the restaurant, dishes in tow, coffee sloshing from side to side, gravy sliding to the edge of the plate while catching up on the latest gossip with customers . . . it's all in a day's work. The body and mind work together like a machine. Her mind instantly computes, tallies, and prioritizes while her eyes scan the room for drink refills. Fast waitresses can make two to three times more money than slower ones simply because they are serving more customers in the same amount of time. It's all about turnover. Time flies as their coffee-stained aprons swell with small bills forming bulges in places you normally wouldn't want them. If everything goes off without a hitch, they feel a sense of pride because they have managed a situation that most people would find too difficult to handle. After a Saturday night rush at the Pie 'n Burger, an observant customer told Jodell, "My God, you are absolutely fabulous."

Once her customers leave, her day isn't over. Almost a quarter of the job is side work, which consists of scrubbing, slicing, sweeping, wiping, refilling, and restocking sticky condiments. Sometimes, it's not until after she sits down to balance her checks that she be-

JODELL KASMARSIK, PIE 'N BURGER, PASADENA, CALIFORNIA

gins to feel her feet throb. While she's working she's usually too busy notice the physical toll the day has taken on her body. Rachel DeCarlo, who worked the graveyard shift at the Sittons North Hollywood Diner for thirteen years from the age of sixty-four to seventy-seven, said, "Of course I have the aches and pains of old age. When it's a busy day, I go home and I practically die. But I enjoy it when we're busy. I think it's exciting. Last Sunday I was so tired from my Saturday night shift I didn't even get dressed. But I feel better after I rest, and then I'm ready to go back and do it again."

Emotional Labor

The flip side of physical labor is what the sociologist Arlie Hochschild calls "emotional labor." Customers can be difficult to please. Some people threaten to send their food back if it's not exactly the way they ordered it, while the next table needs coddling and constant care. Skilled waitresses can anticipate what a customer expects out them. It's a lot of babysitting, making a waitress somewhat of an actress because she must change roles from table to table. Every waitress has to learn to manage the balance between being nice and being real. Most operate from a middle ground so if a waitress is having a bad day she can be emotionally removed. In most service jobs, employees get the same wage no matter what their attitude is. For the waitress, who relies mainly on her tips, how she handles her emotional labor hits her right where it counts—in her pocketbook.

The most natural-acting waitresses generally pull in better tips and make connections with the regulars. It's painfully obvious when a waitress is uncomfortable and is attempting to be witty or humorous. Most people can see right through her insincerity. But not all diner patrons want a nice waitress. William Foote Whyte, a sociologist who wrote a book on the restaurant industry in 1948, quoted a customer: "I've been coming here for over ten years and I doubt if the waitresses have ever said ten civil words to me. I get a kick out of Mary.

She reminds me of my old lady. They don't put up with nothing. I get treated the same here as I do at home." Brit Meschnark, a waitress who worked with her aunt, Susan Thurmond, one of the top-grossing waitresses at the Rainbow, said, "Susan's mean. She's mean as murder and the customers love it." During the lunch rush Susan mistakenly ordered a customer's eggs over-medium instead of scrambled. When she delivered the eggs he pointed out her mistake. Susan picked up his fork, broke up the eggs, and said, "Well they're scrambled now." And walked away. Instead of reporting her to the manager, he thought it was funny and left her a five-dollar tip.

RACHEL DECARLO, SITTONS NORTH HOLLYWOOD DINER, NORTH HOLLYWOOD, CALIFORNIA

Susan Thurmond

Rainbow | Henderson, Nevada

I was raised in the food industry. My parents owned the A&W. It was my first waitressing job. I worked as a carhop on roller skates. That wasn't easy. I had a lot of accidents. The worst one was probably when I hit my breast on the car mirror and the food slid off the tray and went everywhere. After that, I wore shoes.

I'm at work to make money so I usually don't take breaks. I don't like standing around. Nowadays a lot of people say, "I'm in the union. That's not my job" or "I'm jeopardizing somebody else's job if I sweep up the floor," or "I need to call the porter." . . . Personally I think that's crap. Mom didn't raise us that way. When you're at work, I don't care what it is, if it needs to be done—just do it.

I ended up becoming a union steward at the Rainbow. I was talked into it, at first I didn't want to do it, but then I started getting into it. I was learning about stuff you can and can't do, but they were doing anyway. Newcomers come in and don't want to pay $32.50 a month for their dues and since this is a "right-to-work" state, you don't have to pay your dues and you still get all the benefits, so they're thinking why should I pay if I get it for free? Well enough of you freebies do that and we've got no union. You know, it's just that simple.

If you're a good waitress, you can get away with just about anything. You can make mistakes and if you apologize the right way, they'll still love you and they'll still tip. Some girls think because they're young and pretty they can make better tips than the older waitresses. At first, they might do well, because they have a great figure, and a pretty face . . . but honestly, I don't care how cute or gorgeous you are, if you're not a good waitress, it doesn't last long. You know the customers get bored with that too. They'd rather have the older, slightly overweight waitress who can do the job right. I never used my sexuality because my personality was just naturally bold. As I got older, I made more money because I had more call parties (regular customers). I worked at the Rainbow for almost twenty-five years and it was all locals. Everybody knew ya, so it was different from working at the tourists' places, which I don't think I could ever do.

Dolores Jeanpierre

Ole's Waffle Shop | Alameda, California

My name is Dolores Jeanpierre. I'm Creole. I was born in 1951. I grew up picking cotton when I was ten years old in New Roads, Louisiana. It's a small town about ninety minutes outside of New Orleans. We had five stoplights, one hospital, one high school, and no movie theater.

I started waitressing in 1974. I was the first black waitress in Alameda. Two years ago I was voted the best waitress in the city by *Alameda Magazine*. That's pretty amazing, because Alameda had no blacks or Mexicans when I first started. It's much more diverse now.

I took some time off of waitressing to be a bail bondsman. I've had that business for about twenty-five years. When I came back to waitressing, my son Travis said, "Mom, you're a business woman, why do you want to go and carry plates again?" I said, "Ain't nowhere in the world I can go with my paycheck and three days of tips and make $700, nowhere. I couldn't even make that in an office job."

I love to dress for work. I wear something different almost everyday. My customers say, "I've never seen you wear the same thing twice." I've worn a flower in my hair for over thirty years. I wear them everywhere I go. I have every color you can imagine.

I've only had one hostile customer in the last eleven years and it happened just recently. He said I was the worst waitress he had ever had in his life. There was a confusion with his order so I fixed it and came back and said, "Here. No charge." But I guess there was a language barrier (he spoke Spanish) and he thought I said, "Here, cry-baby." He was furious. Once I understood why he was mad, I tried to explain to him what happened, but he didn't believe me. I would never say that to a stranger. I *would* say it to a regular though. Ole's is just that type of place. We joke around a lot. But, see, this is why I don't work weekends. It's mostly tourists and those people are from hell. I like working during the week with my regulars. They're the best part of the job.

I've owned my home for twenty-four years and I drive a 2005 Seville. I've had Cadillacs all my life. I also like to collect old cars. I've got a '68 Buick Skylark. This year, I'm going to be in two car shows. My Buick is powder blue, with a black hard top and the interior is all original. I have a good life.

Jodell Kasmarsik

Pie 'n Burger | Pasadena, California

I've been waitressing for over fifty-two years. I've been here at the Pie 'n Burger forty years. I started when I was seventeen at Van De Kamps. They hired me to cut their pie, and then one night he needed a waitress. My maiden name was Bently and so he said, "Ms. Bently, take the floor!" Back then we had three tables. Now I could run this whole place by myself.

Probably about 75 percent of our customers are regulars. They keep coming back, sometimes two and three times a day. They love the place. It's like a small town in here. I'm in my fourth generation of my customers. I started out with the grandparents and then the parents and then the children and then the grandchildren. It's fantastic.

The regulars are great because most of them have a lot of patience. They say, "Oh, take your time. We're not going anywhere. We'll wait for you." I appreciate it when they say that. I tell them, "I might be a day older, but I'll get to ya."

Most of them order the same thing everyday, but sometimes they want to change their order and I say, "You're going to be sorry if you change, you won't like it. And sure enough they change and they'll say, "You know I don't like it, bring me a cheeseburger. I tell 'em, "See you've got to listen to Mom." I'm Mom.

In all the years I've been here, I can count on one hand all the times I've called in sick and I'd have three or four [fingers] left over. I don't care if I have a backache or a sore foot. I just come to work. I had gotten ill one evening and I had to go home at six o'clock and left the other girl working by herself and when I came back the next day, my boss says, "Why did you check out at six o'clock?" I said, "Well, your warhorse was down. I had to go home but the warhorse is here today and I'm raring to go."

Well, my very favorite story is about the pens. People come up to the register to write a check and they don't have a pen, so they ask to borrow mine. But if I don't stand there and watch them they walk away with it. It's an honest mistake that we all do. So one night when I came home from work, Lilly, my dog—she's a whippet—

she found a pen and chewed it up, so I brought that in thinking, "Oh this is wonderful. They'll never take this pen." Sure enough, someone took it. I told the story in an article in the *Los Angeles Times* and people started sending my pens back. Some said they didn't take a pen but they're sending me pens anyway and one customer brought in two cases of Papermate pens. But someday I hope to find my pen that Lilly chewed up. It's a running joke here at the diner. So when I got a new car last year, I had to change the plates, and I changed the plates to say, "Got A Pen?"

Waitressing is great. You're never broke. You've always got money. I bought a home, my hobby is antiquing, my home is full. And I love flowering and my garden is beautiful. I'll be seventy in December [2006], and people ask me when I'm going to retire but I say, "Why should I retire? It's fun coming to work and I get to visit with all of you." But when the time comes I'll be okay financially. I have invested in mutuals through the years and in other things, like

my antiques. I always seem to know ahead of time what's going to be collectible and what's not. I've sold some of my collections and done real well so I'll be just fine.

Rachel DeCarlo

Sittons North Hollywood Diner | North Hollywood, California

I've been waitressing since October 1943. It was a coffee shop for soldiers in Fort Bliss, Texas. I was thirteen and my parents were farmers and needed money, so I quit school and went to work. I lied about my age. It was wartime so they hired me. The job came easy to me, even though I didn't have any experience. The first time I got a tip I didn't know what it was. I thought the officer had left his change and I told my coworker and she said, "I thought you were an experienced waitress?" I was scared, I needed my job, so I said, "Yes, I am. Is something wrong?" "Well, no. But an experienced waitress knows that this tip is for her." Well I've been a waitress ever since.

At Fort Bliss, we went to food handlers' school for six weeks. You had to have a health certificate to work in the post. We learned to serve, carry glasses, to not put your fingers in the food, to not stand around, or wipe your face, and touch your hair while you're working. Tell that to younger waitresses and they say, 'Oh, don't be so fussy.'

I worked Jewish delis in Los Angeles until about fifteen years ago. I loved them because if you gave good service you got good tips. Now, the deli's are too fast for me at my age. I worked grave-yard here at Sittons for about fourteen years, to pace myself. About six years ago I thought I was going to retire . . . my hands are getting bad with arthritis. But I still have my memory and I keep all my orders in my head. I'm seventy-seven.

I was a union waitress for thirty-five years. I'm retired from it now, but I will get health insurance benefits for the rest of my life. The younger waitresses I worked with are working until they find a better job. They think they're going to find something better, but they're not. Maybe nowadays, but when I was young there were fewer opportunities. I've worked with waitresses who've left to do office work and they come back to waitressing because they make more money.

I'm full-blooded Mexican. My regulars like to sit with me because I speak Spanish. Younger waitresses flirt with customers thinking they'll get more money, but it's really about service. One

customer who comes to me knows he'll get fresh coffee. Some waitresses will make several pots at a time. They don't care if the coffee sits there for hours and get stale. Or they will mix old coffee with a fresh pot. I tell the other waitresses, 'Don't touch my coffee pot.' I have a regular who comes in everyday at 5 am and he drinks decaf, so I don't make any decaf until right before he comes in so he gets a fresh cup. That's important. Also, I warm the cup for my special customers because it's the first cup that they look forward to. Most people don't understand what we do. Waitressing is a dying art.

The Regulars

It all starts with a cup of coffee. Watered down, freshly brewed, or gray with age, coffee is usually the first thing a waitress serves. If they're regulars, she knows whether they take it black, with extra creamers, or if they prefer Sweet 'n Low over Splenda. Like a doctor's stethoscope, her coffee pot is an instrument that reveals intimate details about her customers. It tells her whether they are lactose intolerant, diabetic, or if they avoid caffeine all together. In any form, coffee is the quintessential tonic of the roadside restaurant and an entry point into a relationship that, for many waitresses, can last more than thirty years.

"You can read a person by the first cup of coffee you serve them," said Carol Jimenez, the counter waitress at Sears Fine Foods. "It doesn't seem like much at first. You can talk to people for a year and not even know their name. And then all the sudden one day you say, 'What was your name?' And then it's like you've known them forever. You know all about them and they know all about you. You don't just go up to someone and say, 'Hey, I want to be your friend now.' Or, 'Let's go have coffee sometime.' You don't do that. The relationship just happens."

It's different from a traditional friendship. Waitresses and regulars build relationships through a progression of seemingly insignificant moments that develop into a connection unlike any other.

Fueled by food, conversation, companionship, and trust, this bond takes years, sometimes decades to form, and the rewards—although piecemeal—are undeniable.

In most coffee shops the counter functions as a small, makeshift community where everybody knows your name—*Cheers* without the liquor. Customers bring warmth, character, and vitality to the workplace and become extended family members to each other and to the restaurant staff. One regular at Betsy's Pancake House in New Orleans said, "It's like sitting on your front porch with your neighbors." They pass the time arguing over politics, telling jokes, swapping war stories, sharing family sagas, and spreading local gossip. Many career waitresses have waited on three generations of the same family. Just like a long lost aunt or a distant cousin, waitresses watch their regulars' kids grow up. They attend birthday parties and graduations, and when regulars get sick, their favorite waitress is there, visiting them in the hospital with a positive attitude. Kathleen Woody of Ryan's in Florence, Alabama, said, "It's amazing how we touch people. We brighten their lives. One of my customers told me they wouldn't have gotten through their chemotherapy without me."

Regulars come as they are. They show up in every shape, age, color, creed, class, profession, and subculture: from farmers to

CAROL JIMENEZ AND JOE HERNANDEZ,
SEARS FINE FOOD, SAN FRANCISCO,
CALIFORNIA

(LEFT) "MEDICINE MAN," IRON SKILLET
TRUCK STOP, KINGMAN, ARIZONA

gang members, immigrant day laborers to elected officials, cow-boys to cab drivers, they make the diner a daily part of their lives. Walk into almost any hometown diner and you can find a collection of characters that represent a broad range of American culture. It's the melting pot America claims to be, all happening under one roof. Some regulars have idiosyncrasies that only their waitress can satisfy. Take, for instance, the regular known as the "Medicine Man." He will eat his food at the Iron Skillet Truck Stop only in a Styrofoam container.

The widowed often use the diner as a social outlet and their waitress may be the only person they talk to that day, so it can't just be any waitress, it has to be the one who recognizes them as soon as they walk through the door. Faye Blackwell, who has been wait-ressing for over thirty years, said, "To my customers, I'm a psychia-trist, a nurse, a mama, a grandmama. . . . I'm whatever they need me to be."

When a waitress leaves the restaurant or changes her schedule, her customers feel it the most. Virginia Brandon, who worked days at the Rainbow in Henderson, Nevada, for thirteen years, said, "The regulars eat the same thing everyday. I'd see them come in, I'd hang their ticket. By the time they'd sit, I'd put the plate down in front of them." When Virginia moved from days to the swing shift, her regulars were disoriented and confused. The new waitress who took over Virginia's shift asked one of her regulars, "What are you gonna have?" He looked at her with fear in eyes: "I don't know! Where's Virginia? She always orders my food for me."

The former Kentucky senator Walter Baker has been coming to George J's in Glasgow, Kentucky, since the 1960s, and he loved be-ing waited on by his favorite waitress, Maye Elmore, now retired. He said, "Maye's irreplaceable. Her personality, the way she looks at you . . . if there was something she didn't think was up to snuff, she'd let you know about it. It's almost like your mom or your wife.

SENATOR WALTER A.
BAKER, GEORGE J'S,
GLASGOW, KENTUCKY

I was on the state supreme court. I served during the Reagan administration on Secretary Weinberger's staff and was the state senator for five terms. When I had to spend time in Washington, the thing I missed the most about Glasgow was George J's. Coming in here, having coffee, seeing Maye, seeing my friends. And Maye was always here. The wonderful thing about coming to George J's for coffee every morning was if there was any news you needed to catch up on, Maye could always get you reliably informed as to what was going on. Or if [there was] somebody you needed to contact and you couldn't locate them, you would ask Maye and she would know where they were. Many places don't have the uniqueness and the sense of community, the sense of friendliness and family that George J's has and Maye was principally responsible for that."

Politicians love diners because they offer a ready-made portrait of the American people. After the devastation of Hurricane Katrina, President Bush ate at Betsy's Pancake House in New Orleans and made a long-awaited appearance to the locals who had lost faith in his abilities to come to their aid. Betsy McDaniel, the owner, asked Sharon Bruno to wait on President Bush. "About ten minutes before he came in," Sharon said, "Miss Betsy was in the back cutting bread and the Secret Service went back there and said, 'Miss Betsy, in about ten minutes we're going to bring the president in here to eat.' Betsy says, 'Okay.' And she keeps cutting her bread. He leans over and says, 'Miss Betsy, I'm serious. We have to get your staff together and tell them, no cell phones, no cameras, and no one is to approach the table unless they are told.' She stops and looks up at

SHARON BRUNO
WITH MAYOR
RAY NAGIN AND
PRESIDENT
GEORGE W. BUSH.
COURTESY OF
SHARON BRUNO.

PAT DERMATIS AND COWBOY, SIP 'N BITE, BALTIMORE, MARYLAND

him and says, 'Why are you bringing him in here?' He said, 'Because we've been coming in here for the past ten days. This is a locally owned small business, basically all family members work here, and you opened eight months after the storm. The president needs to see and feel this. This is what New Orleans is about.'"

Patti Dermatis of the Sip 'n Bite has her faithful regulars. She said, "When you walk through the door they're just sitting there waiting for you. When someone else tries to serve them, they say, 'Just give me coffee. I'm waiting for Patti to come in.'" At Sharkey's in Gardnerville, Nevada, Esther Paul said, "I've had some custom-

ers who have waited for over two hours to sit with me. I have others who drive from San Francisco [a four-hour drive] regularly to see me." Waitresses play such a critical role in the lives of their regulars it's not uncommon for them to leave their life savings to their favorite waitress when they die.

Regulars become such a part of the restaurant family that if they haven't come in for a while, the restaurant owners will call them at home to check to make sure they are okay. Some waitresses nurse their regulars in their homes when they get too old to come in. And when regulars die, the whole restaurant goes into mourn-

ing. "The last time I cried at work was when we lost Kendall," Susan Thurmond remembered, "I waited on him for over twenty years. He ate bacon over medium and wheat toast or biscuits and gravy, depending on his mood. He died from emphysema. It just hit me really hard. I mean he was just one of those people you love. You could say anything to him. We'd see each other everyday, sometimes twice a day, and when he got sick, I had a feeling something was wrong, so I called Neddy [his wife] because I hadn't seen Kendall. I said, "How's Kendall?" She said, "He's not doing so good . . ." It was about eight thirty at night and I said, "Do you mind if I come over?" I went and visited with him . . . and sure enough, he died the next morning. So I was real blessed to get to spend some time with him."

Not all regulars are pleasant to be around. Some are cranky, others are lousy tippers, and there are many who are difficult to please. But a good waitress will take the time to try to turn a cus-

tomer around. One regular named Gerdie ate at Miz Brown's Feed Bag in San Francisco for years. Sallie Power remembered her well. "She was about four feet tall and she had a cane that was two feet tall. She was the cutest little thing, but, boy, was she mean. When she needed a coffee refill, she would bang her silverware on her coffee cup so loud the entire restaurant could hear it." After about ten years of that, Sallie decided she was going to win Gerdie over. She asked her, "Why are you in such a hurry?" Gerdie just ignored her. But Sallie tried to talk to her a little more every day and she finally got the story. Gerdie said in an irritated tone, "I'm going to bingo and I don't want to be late!" From then on Sallie gave Gerdie her own teapot with coffee in it so that she could do her own refill. "After that, she was a sweetheart, she just loved everybody. It was like she was a new person because someone took the time to understand her. When she turned a hundred years old, we threw her a big party at the restaurant with streamers and everything. She was so excited."

Whatever their attitude, regulars help keep coffee shops recession-proof. They come in every day, regardless of the weather, the traffic, or even the threat of a terrorist attack. After 9/11, the restaurant industry in southern Nevada was hit so hard that for two months the IRS allowed service workers to cut their tip allocation on their taxes in half. Instead of paying out eight percent of their income, they were taxed only four percent. But Virginia said that the recession hadn't bothered their business at the Rainbow a bit because they had all their faithful customers. "Same people, everyday. Thank God. Nobody got laid off, nobody got their hours cut, and our business was as good as it ever was."

Esther had the most regular customers at Sharkey's because she knew how to treat her special customers. Hidden in the back room, she had a stash of doggy bags full of leftover beef rib bones for her canine-loving patrons, and she always had treats for her customers. She said, "We don't have toppings for our ice cream. So years ago I asked Sharkey if I could bring in my own chocolate syrup from home. He said, 'You can bring anything you want for your people. Just put it away so that nobody else uses it.' And every Friday my regular comes in, and has his chocolate topping. And that means so much to him that I thought enough to bring it from home when he knows we don't carry it." Esther's manager, Mashelle Begovich, said, "She's spoiled them so much. If they come in and don't see her working, they'll turn around and walk out."

Man J. Kim understood the power of longstanding waitresses when he bought Sears Fine Food in San Francisco. Before he purchased Sears, it had been owned by the same family for over sixty years, and many of the waitresses who worked there were older and had a loyal following. After Kim purchased Sears, he temporarily closed it for renovations, but when it reopened, he rehired most of the older waitresses because he knew that they were extremely valuable to his business; without them, his customer base would be cut in half.

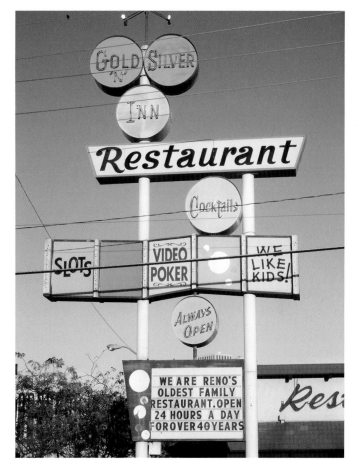

GOLD 'N SILVER RESTAURANT, RENO, NEVADA

ESTHER AND SHARKEY IN THE BACK. COURTESY OF ESTHER PAUL.

Regulars are not only good for business, they also make the waitress's job easier. "It's a routine," said Georgina Moore of the Gold 'n Silver in Reno, Nevada. "All I say is, 'The usual?' and they say, 'Yeah.' And that's to 90 percent of the customers who come in here. We know when it's nine o'clock because Frank and Pete come in and we know when it's nine thirty because Larry and Bob come in and our day goes by that. I have a gentleman who I wait on in the morning that I've waited on for twenty-three years, who has never changed his order." Knowing what they eat helps cut down her physical labor immensely. If she's in a hurry, she doesn't have to tip toe around their emotions. And when the regulars get impatient, she can put them in their place. Georgina calls lunchtime at the Gold 'n Silver the "ulcer hour." She said, "Everybody drives a half hour and has ten minutes to eat and we can't get the food out of the kitchen fast enough. It's stressful. Five minutes after ordering, the customer will say, 'Where's my food? I've only got ten more minutes.' I have to tell all of them, 'Now look at this restaurant, every table in here is full, they all want to eat now, too. You aren't the only one here, you'll just have to wait.' I don't care if they're a senator or if they dig ditches for a living. I treat everyone the same. I feel like I know them all so personally and they know so much about me, too. I can say what I need to and they're not offended."

People let their guard down in diners. They spill their secrets and reveal personal details about their lives. Waitresses know a lot about their regulars' personal lives and they depend on her discretion. Some waitresses say when they see the senators, governors, judges, and attorneys they serve in the diner on television they don't even recognize them because of "the way they talk in here." Susan said, "Some customers are extra nice to us and they tip us well, because we overhear *everything* and we see a lot. Some of them come in half lit with a woman who isn't his wife and we give 'em that look the next day."

It's a win-win relationship. In return for their care, coddling, pampering, and discretion, career waitresses reap many rewards. Regulars give them discounted or free legal services, car repair, therapy, and medical care. They give her suckers or gum to help her quit smoking, they bring in cold medicine if they hear her sniffling, and during the holidays and on her birthday they give her extra money. When Jo Ann Archer, a waitress at the Crystal Diner in Lawrenceville, New Jersey, fell and hurt herself and wasn't able to work, her customers made a collection and paid her mortgage. "But I've been here forever," she said, "We take care of each other. They're like my family."

The Greek philosopher Epicurus said, "When it comes to happiness, *who* you eat with is more important than *what* you eat." In most greasy spoons, people don't usually come for the food. It's the environment that attracts them: an unpretentious, informal place with service tailored for their special needs. It's where regular folks can come to grab a bite and just be. They don't have to talk or be polite. They become a part of the community just by being there. Jean Joseph said, "Someday we're going to have a sign made that says, 'Nobody but the nicest people walk through this door.' If they're not, they are by the time they leave here."

JO ANN ARCHER, CRYSTAL DINER, LAWRENCEVILLE, NEW JERSEY

GEORGINA MOORE, GOLD 'N SILVER RESTAURANT, RENO, NEVADA

Georgina Moore

Gold 'n Silver | Reno, Nevada

I started waiting tables in 1971. It was three buildings down the street from here, at Jerry's restaurant. I liked the job okay, but I just knew waitressing wasn't what I was going to do with my life. I took a two-month leave of absence to do secretarial work. That was completely different, sitting down all the time. . . . I had no one to talk to. I didn't like it. I didn't even last two months. Plus I made a lot more money waitressing. I don't understand why people choose jobs like that. They pay less than waitressing. I figured, I'm working for the money, so I may as well go where it is.

To me, waitressing is still hard but not as hard. It's gotten easier over the years because I'm older now. I don't put up with as much as I used to when I was younger, because I didn't know anything back then, but after waitressing thirty years, I'm more secure now. My customers know how to act because they know what I expect. I don't beat around the bush, I'll tell a customer anything. I'll tell them right to their face if they smell bad, if they look like they've been out all night or if they're a pain in the ass. I'm honest and I think they appreciate it. I never used to be this way—it's just been the last eight to ten years, I think.

At the Gold 'n Silver, it's mostly regular customers. I wait on a

FAYE BLACKWELL, TRIO RESTAURANT, WASHINGTON, D.C.

round table every morning—they're called my million-dollar table because the senators, doctors, and attorneys all come . . . there's about twenty-five to thirty of them. I wait on them every single morning, even holidays. And I have to remember who wants decaf, who wants regular, who wants rye, who wants butter and dietary syrup, and who wants their syrup heated; there's one who wants one piece of wheat buttered and the other piece dry, another wants blackberry jam instead of anything else and then there's the one who wants me to cut up their doughnut . . . honestly! But to me it's easy because I've done it for so long.

Faye Blackwell

Trio Restaurant | Washington, D.C.

I moved here from Richmond, Virginia. I could type, but other than that, I had no skills and I had three children to raise by myself. In 1969 I went to the employment bureau and decided to look for office work. They said, "Forget it you'll never raise three children being a secretary. Go get a waitressing job." I thought, "You're crazy." But I listened to the lady. I went and got a waitressing job the next day. And she was right. I was able to raise my children fine without any help.

I made great money, immediately. I made so much money at the end of the night when everyone would count their tips and say what they had made, I would never tell anyone what I made because I didn't want them to feel bad. I'd say, "I don't like to say what I made, I think it's bad luck."

I love waitressing. I worked five straight years, double shifts, and never missed a day. Actually one day a server didn't come in and I worked the whole place myself. The owner had the good sense not to talk to me so I could keep my thoughts collected. He didn't say anything to me until the end of the day and someone's cell phone went off and he asked me, "What was that? Your pacemaker? [laughing]."

If a customer comes in three times, I consider them a regular. By then I know their name, what they eat, if their mother is ill, or if they need surgery. Usually when I see sadness in their eyes—that's when I try to touch on them. I ask, "Do you feel well?" And then when I see them again, I check in to see if things are better.

Working in this neighborhood [Dupont Circle in Washington, D.C.] has really taken a toll on me emotionally because this is predominately a gay area. I've lost so many of my customers to AIDS. It's just been heartbreaking, I started here in the eighties when the treatment for AIDS wasn't very effective and people were dying every month. It was very painful to see them go. I would be there at the hospices to visit them. I lost one customer not too long ago. His name was Cody. I think he'd just turned forty. I was actually holding his hand when he passed away in the hospital. I have a little urn on my mantle at home with his ashes in it.

I got a mother's day card from Cody every year. He'd make me one on his computer. He was such a funny little devil. He painted his hair purple one time, green another. He had the funniest little laugh. And he was so tiny. He wasn't any bigger than I am and I just kind of felt like mothering him. When he wasn't eating, I tried to find ways to get him to eat. I said, "If you don't eat your food, I'm going to put it in the back of the kitchen and you'll have to eat when you come back before you can have anything else. I tried to coax him all the time, "Please, just eat one more bite, one more piece." But he just lost his appetite.

His parents disowned him at sixteen. He was very sad about it. They were from Texas, and it was the saddest thing when they came and saw him dying. He was on life support. I felt sorry for them because they missed out on having a beautiful son. Many of my customers are gay and I find that a lot of them are shunned by their families. How could a parent shun a child for being gay? It's beyond me. I just don't understand it. I'm just grateful for the time I got to spend with them. It makes me feel good to think I am making someone else's life a little bit easier. It's why I love the job so much. That's the bonus of doing this work, for me.

My daughter was thinking of getting a tattoo for her birthday and she asked me what kind of tattoo I would get if I got one. I said, "*Born to serve*. Right across my arm."

FAYE'S REGULAR, CODY (ON THE RIGHT). COURTESY OF FAYE BLACKWELL.

Maye Elmore

George J's | Glasgow, Kentucky

We had a farm on Tobacco Road near Lucas, Kentucky. There were about twenty acres. We grew tobacco, corn, hay, and wheat. My momma died when I was about six years old and my father remarried. After a while, she had enough of the farm and we moved to Louisville. My stepmother was working here at George J's restaurant and I started working here around 1938. I worked here for over fifty years. I never worked at any other restaurant. They wouldn't let me leave anyway. They had a fit because I started working part-time. People are really nice to you if you're good to them. Some waitresses would say, "I want to know why they think so much of you and don't care about us." And I'd say, "Well, I guess it's just the way I treat 'em."

I had my customers spoiled. I knew what they wanted. I knew what they drank. I never did go ask them. I'd just take it to them, and that was it. There were some customers from out of town who'd sit in the back with the regulars. I got their water and brought it back and I knew one who always wanted coffee as soon as he sat down. So I served it and some of them other guys said, "How in the hell do you know to bring him coffee? Why don't we get any coffee?" I said, "Well, I don't know y'all. I know him. I know he wants his coffee." One of 'em said, "Well, I want coffee too." I said, "Well alright, then you'll get it."

I had four men that came in from Louisville on a Saturday. Me and my daughter were working. Most of the staff had gone home and we was fixing to go home and here come these guys. One of them said, "Can't y'all cook us something to eat?" and Larry said, "Yes. We'll cook it." So we turned the grill back on and fixed it for 'em. So they sat and eat and talked until about three o'clock in the morning when I asked them if they'd had enough. They said, "Yeah, what time do y'all go home?" I said, "Well, we were sup-

posed to have been home a long time ago. But we stay for anybody who comes in and wants to eat. They said, "Well, we better go." He tipped us twenty dollars. I thanked him and said, "That's a whole lot for a tip." And he said, "I'll tell you what. You don't get a good waitress like y'all. Now when we come back to Glasgow, we'll be back in here." They was gone about two months and then one Saturday afternoon they come in and I said, "Lord have mercy! Who are you all?" They said, "Honey, we're your baby!"

SHARON BRUNO, BETSY'S PANCAKE HOUSE, NEW ORLEANS, LOUISIANA

Sharon Bruno

Betsy's Pancake House | New Orleans, Louisiana

I was born and raised in New Orleans. My dad passed away when I was five. My mom was a hard worker. She was a waitress herself. She never encouraged me to wait tables. She said, "Stay in school, be a doctor or a lawyer. Don't be a waitress."

Even though waitressing is tough, it has its rewards. When I worked at the Fairmont Hotel in New Orleans they needed a bus girl and then soon after that I started waitressing. I've met Mohammed Ali, Tom Jones, Tony Bennett, Lou Rawls, and Sonny and Cher.

Working in a hotel is really different. Where I work now, it's all locals. In the hotel business, it's all tourists. But even at the Fairmont, I met some nice people. Once a customer sent me a ticket to Indianapolis for his birthday party. I didn't know him from Adam, but his mom sent me a ticket for his birthday party and said will you come? I said, "Sure."

Ninety-five percent of my customers are regulars. We have a lot of cab drivers, lawyers, and construction workers. When I waited on President Bush, Mayor Ray Nagin came in with him. He's a very nice guy and now when he comes in, he always sits with me.

I'll be fifty-eight in February [2008] but I think the exercise we get here keeps me young. We put a pedometer on us one day to see how far we walk and we found out that we walk about nine and a half miles every day. Back and forth, carrying heavy trays and glasses. I'm here Monday to Friday and we work ten-hour shifts. I start at 5 am. We're all family here, even though we're not blood related. But I see them more than I see my family. When I come in the morning I say, "I'm home!"

SHARON BRUNO, BETSY'S PANCAKE HOUSE, NEW ORLEANS, LOUISIANA

All in the Family

Restaurant workers are devoted to the business. Even in the midst of chaos, on the days where everything goes wrong, they find a way to keep going. Irregular hours, irritable customers, and temperamental cooks don't scare them away. They enjoy the pressure of working in a time-sensitive environment, and they like the fact that every day offers a new set of challenges. They can't stomach sitting all day at a desk job, waiting for a paycheck every two weeks. "It gets in your blood," said Kathleen Woody of Florence, Alabama, "After that, there's no going back."

At their best, restaurants are reliable and consistent, churning out tasty meals and friendly service. At their worst, they are sluggish, neglectful, and unpredictable places that dish out inedible slop. The good, the bad, and the ugly can all happen in the same diner (often in the same hour) because success depends on so many variables and so many people; it's difficult to keep everything and everyone on course. Adding to the challenge, restaurants are one of the few industries that merge production and service in the same place. Most businesses either provide a service or manufacture a product that is packaged in one location and then sold in another. Few industries create a perishable product to be delivered on the premises, using two modes of production, operating in the same space.

KATHLEEN WOODY AS A YOUNGER WAITRESS.
COURTESY OF KATHLEEN WOODY.

Restaurants are divided between the dining room (the front of the house) and the kitchen (the back of the house). The front area is staged for presentation. Despite the casual environment of the coffee shop, a show is performed for customers. When a waitress is in the kitchen with the line cooks and the dishwashers, she is at liberty to relax, be furious, complain about her worst customers, or boast about the money she's making. In the back she can do the unmentionables—nibble on food, lounge, touch her face, and inspect the food she's serving for wayward strands of hair. A newer waitress may use the back as a refuge. She may storm into the kitchen and cry when she's been confronted with one too many irate customers. The back area becomes a psychological space where she can just be, without worrying that someone may be watching her. It's much brighter in the kitchen, and a radio is usually playing anything from classic rock to Spanish pop. Walking into the back is like entering a different world, where the production of grease, stains, and spills is characteristic of the space. It's a utilitarian, monochromatic world; everything seems to match and any random color is a welcome contrast. Shiny silver metal is offset by harsh sterile whites, and vented tubes channel odors and smoke outside. The temperature is usually much warmer in the kitchen, and in the dead of summer, a sweltering, wall-sweating heat is only for those who can take it. The back is designed for moments when everything goes awry; it's fast-paced, sloppy, and the most unrefined area in the restaurant. Like the backstage of a theater, the kitchen is where the dirt (both psychological and physical) gets tossed, managed, cleaned up, and prepared for presentation.

Restaurants run like well-oiled machines. With such a tightly integrated system, one missing gear can set off a chain reaction that ripples throughout the entire restaurant. Despite how simple it appears—a customer sits down and orders food that is delivered within minutes—the system has very little room for error, so it is critical to have a solid, dependable staff. Getting food to the table is a combined effort among the staff that requires skill, patience, coordination, camaraderie, support, and trust. With time *not* on her side, a waitress needs to be able to depend on her coworkers at

MISS ROXIE BURTON, FLORIDA AVENUE GRILL, WASHINGTON, D.C.

a moment's notice. Her station must be amply stocked so that all of her tools are ready to grab and go without delay. At the end of the shift, most waitresses are required to tip out the staff, which usually includes the busser, the hostess, and sometimes the cooks and the dishwashers. If everyone performs well, she makes money and everybody gets a taste. Her busser is her most important ally, serving and refilling water and coffee, clearing dishes, and checking in with customers. Bussers hustle more than anyone else in the restaurant and usually get up to 20 percent of the waitress's tips. The amount she gives to the busser, however, is ultimately up to her. This can cause a rift in some restaurants where lazy bussers leave extra work for the waitresses. Susan Thurmond of the Rainbow in Henderson, Nevada, said, "I usually tip out very well, but if my bus kid sucks, he ain't gonna get nothing."

Sibling Rivalry

In longstanding coffee shops where there is little turnover among the staff, the restaurant starts to feel like home. Carol Jimenez at Sears Fine Food in San Francisco remembered, "Years ago we had carpets on the floor and it gave the place a close, cozy feeling—it was like your living room. It was that kind of an atmosphere. But God, the girls used to fight and the language . . . you wouldn't believe! There was always somebody fighting with somebody and holding a grudge. Everybody has their own quirk, and as soon as you get into a fight the first thing that person is going to do is slam you with it. I don't care what it is, they're just gonna nail you. But at the same time we got along 99 percent of the time. We were all so close we really kind of gelled as a family."

One of the most important relationships among staff members is between the waitress and the cook. Carol said, "The cooks here at Sears are amazing. This one cook could take ten omelet orders and remember everything you yelled at him, and then have it ready for you in five minutes. I mean we're talking bacon, cheese, avocado . . . everything. If you have really good cooks, you've got the world by the tail."

If cooks and waitresses don't work together, the system grinds to a halt. Say a customer sends the food back and the cook refuses to remake it. The waitress is in a no-win situation. If the cook wasn't there, she could make the order herself, but the cooks guard their domain like a fortress. One waitress admitted, "They're temperamental and they always have an attitude." One day at Sharkey's, the food looked terrible and Esther Paul told the cook, "I wouldn't serve that to a dog." The cook said, "Well, I'm the chef and . . ." Esther interrupted, "I don't care who you are! If the people won't eat it, I won't serve it."

It takes decades for waitresses to get the courage to stand up to the cooks, because they can be intimidating. When Laverne Phillips started out she was working at Bunny's Waffle Shop in San Francisco. She remembered, "I was working the counter for the whole house. It was stressful, because I didn't really know the food, so when I'd have to go pick up my orders, I'd stand at the window and think 'Jesus, is that my order?' and the chef would yell at me, 'TAKE YOUR HAND OFF THAT!' He was so cockeyed and mean I never knew which order was mine. I'd ask and he'd scream at me, 'WHAT, YOU CAN'T SEE?' I thought, Oh, brother, get me out of here."

As in a real family, the ones you love can bring out the best and the worst in you. Battles between waitresses and cooks can escalate to dangerous heights. Careers have ended and lives have been lost in restaurant kitchens. In 1997 a cook shot and killed a waitress after arguing about poached eggs at the Pinecrest Diner in San Francisco. Less than a mile from the Pinecrest, Wilma Mobbs, a waitress at Sears Fine Food, ended her almost fifty-year waitressing career over a side of soggy bacon. She said, "The customer sent it back three times and the cook kept remaking it the same way. The manager did nothing about it, so I walked out and never went back."

Managing the Family

Managers run the business aspect of the restaurant. They work with food distributors to get the best prices; they manage and enforce employee labor schedules; they balance the books and make sure everyone gets paid on time; they keep the equipment and the furniture in good working order; they do all the hiring and firing; and

they try to build a reliable staff so they can spend most of their time in their office doing their work. Spending less time on the floor, however, separates the managers from their staff, both physically and emotionally. As a result they are not included in the group on a sibling level. They are more like parents—respected for their position but kept at a safe distance. The staff looks out for each other and forms a united front that rarely includes management. Virginia Brandon of the Rainbow in Henderson, Nevada, said, "Every time we'd get a new manager who would come in and try to change things, we banded together and held our ground. Either they'd quit or fall in line with us."

In some coffee shops with a veteran wait staff, managers do not hold the same amount of power as office, factory, or retail managers. In many cases, career waitresses have been working at the restaurant longer than the manager. And having a loyal clientele ensures that her customers are there to see her. Working in a tip-based system also gives her more power and control over her salary. Her priority is to please her customers, not her supervisors, so she's really working for herself. When a manager tried to pull rank, one waitress reported saying, "Oh, who cares, what are you going to do? Fire me?" She continued, "If he'd [the manager] threaten to write a waitress up, we'd turn around and look at him, laugh and say, 'Yeah, okay. You go right ahead.'"

Waitresses who tip out their cooks can get them to supply her customers with special orders and larger portions. "To make sure my customers are satisfied, I'll slip a cook a five," one waitress admitted. Over the years, this works in her favor but not necessarily the restaurant's. In an attempt to control the power dynamics, some managers will forbid the wait staff to tip the cooks, especially in the smaller, old-time establishments that still use the wheel instead of computers for placing orders. Without computers, it is nearly impossible to keep track of inventory. In fact, some waitresses admitted that they play dumb by insisting that they can't use a computer (even though they have one at home), and if they are forced to switch, many have threatened to quit.

Although some waitresses confessed to trying to outsmart their managers, most achieved the same respect by following the rules. Sammi DeAngelis of the Seville Diner in East Brunswick, New Jersey, said, "When my boss says 'no substitutions,' I do what he says. He invested the money, it's his business, and I respect that. Some customers come in here and try to manipulate me into giving them what they want. You know, I'd love to give out free food, but this isn't Never-Never land and I'm not Peter Pan."

SAMMI DEANGELIS AND HER MANAGER, SEVILLE DINER, EAST BRUNSWICK, NEW JERSEY

Waitresses such as Sammi who show initiative, drive, and maturity are usually promoted to head waitress. Some are offered a higher hourly wage and given badges with numbers to indicate their position above the other waitresses. But most career waitresses are not social climbers. They couldn't care less about the title of head waitress or even manager. It's already apparent who the head waitresses are. They have the most regular customers, make the most money, and in many cases have been working there the longest. But these women didn't need any promotion. Virginia said, "Because we've been there so long, we didn't feel like waitresses. We felt like we owned the place. You're at work so much, you start to feel like the place just can't go on without you."

Over 90 percent of the waitresses interviewed were offered management positions, but fewer than 5 percent accepted. Based on the waitresses' testimonies, it was evident they didn't think there was much to gain from being a manager. To them, it's an unrewarding job that offers little more than grief from fussy patrons and a staff that doesn't respect them. A waitress-turned-manager would lose the freedom to be herself and wouldn't be able to spend as much time with her regular customers. Managing would require her to be more diplomatic and she would be forced to make decisions that are good for the company but might not be good for the workers. Also, the respect she gets from her employees may not be entirely genuine; she would never know if people are nice to her because they truly like her or because she can give them the schedule they want. Suddenly she's an outsider to the family she has known for many years. Usually the shift in perceived power is not worth the effort. In fact, Esther said, "They couldn't pay me enough to be a manager."

The Rainbow is part of a chain that has several restaurants and managers who move around from property to property. Virginia said, "For a while there was a new manager every six months. We wouldn't even bother to learn their names because we knew they wouldn't stick around. I think some of them are intimidated to be working with older women and teenagers. At our place, there's no middle gap; there's these old women, set in their ways, and these kids who don't want to do anything." When new managers are hired, they usually have to go to the veteran waitress to find out how things should work in the restaurant. The whole concept of manager seems flipped when the workforce ends up training their superiors about the specific needs of the locals, the presentation of the meals, and other issues unique to the restaurant that aren't taught in college hospitality courses. Virginia said, "They asked me to be a manager—several times, as a matter of fact. I remember one time this manager named Cliff was interviewing people for the job. And this guy he interviewed was a good candidate, so he offered it to him. And then, at the last minute, Cliff said, 'Oh, wait a minute.' He picked up the phone, called down to the restaurant, and said, 'Virginia are you sure you don't want this management job?' I said, 'No.' So Cliff told the guy, 'Okay, you've got the job.' So, of course, the new manager came down hating me and he hadn't even met me [laughing]. He didn't last long."

Another reason waitresses don't accept a management position is because, in many cases, they would make less money. In high-end restaurants there is a considerable difference in salary from the dishwasher to the executive chef—especially now that chefs are achieving celebrity status. But in coffee shops, the difference in salary between management and the servers is not as wide as some would think. According to Susan, "It doesn't pay to be a manager." Her sister Lindsay makes about $40,000 waitressing while the managers at her restaurant make only $26,000.

Managing is tough. It's the manager who has to keep the system maintained and lubricated. If the grill breaks, it's the manager who usually has to crawl on the floor looking for pieces of broken equipment. If the dishwasher storms out in protest, the manager can't take a cook or a busser off their duties to help out; instead the manager has to roll up his or her sleeves and get his or her hands scorched in bacteria-killing solutions. The tenuous and precarious nature of the business is something that managers understand all too well. It's in their best interest to support their staff and keep them content so they don't organize a walk out. When Georgina Moore started working in 1971, she was hired as a busser. After about ten minutes on her first day, all the girls got mad and walked off the floor. The manager came to her and said, "Now you're a waitress."

Despite the power struggles, bickering, and dramatic outbursts, most longstanding restaurants have a cohesive, family-like atmosphere among the staff. Managers not only respect their older waitresses, they understand and value their contribution to their business. One of the worst parts of the job is not having medical or retirement benefits. But when longstanding waitresses have health problems, many can depend on their managers to come to their aid. Esther said, "My voice started changing and my manager didn't like the sound of it, so she took me in to see their family doctor. They did x-rays and they found a spot on my lung, so I had to take seventy pills. My medication was $918. Sharkey [the owner] paid for all of my medical bills. He bought my medication and made me take three weeks off to heal. During that time I was off, Sharkey's daughter, Mashelle, who is the manager, came to my house everyday to check in and see how I was doing."

JACKIE ROBINSON, BUSY BEE CAFE, ATLANTA, GEORGIA

JACKIE ROBINSON, BUSY BEE CAFE, ATLANTA, GEORGIA

A good manager recognizes the value of his or her employees. Tracy Gates at the Busy Bee Cafe in Atlanta, Georgia, said, "I invest in my workers." She takes them on vacations every year and pays for everything—including their salary while they're away. "If you don't respect your workers and treat them right," she said, "how can you expect them to stay loyal to you? I do whatever I can for them. I help them pay their bills when they're having a rough time and I give them time off if they need more time with their kids. And in return, I get a healthy, happy workforce. They almost never call in sick and they know they can come to me for anything."

Jackie Robinson

Busy Bee Cafe | Atlanta, Georgia

I've worked at the Busy Bee for almost twenty years. This is one of the best soul food restaurants in Atlanta. We've won lots of awards for our food. We serve fresh vegetables, smoked turkey, chitterlings, ham hocks. . . . Everything is cooked daily from scratch. And people just love our key lime cake and peach cobblers.

A long time ago, I waitressed at Woolworth's department store, but they let me go after about eight months. It was mostly a white place. There were no other black waitresses, only cooks. They didn't like my hair because I wore braids. I don't know why it became a problem later because my hair was in braids when they hired me. But you know, they were a little prejudiced.

Waitressing is really not a hard job. You just try to give people good service and accommodate them in any way you can. When the regulars come, no matter where they sit in the restaurant, even if they're in someone else's section, if they ask for us, we take care of them. A lot of them are clergymen. And you have to be patient with the college students—they can get on your nerves sometimes. I've waited on celebrities too. I waited on Jill Scott and on Puff Daddy or P Diddy, whatever he's calling himself now. Anyway, I was so nervous! I lost it for a minute. I couldn't catch my breath.

We've all been here so long; we're like a big family. And Tracy [the manager] is so good to us. She takes us on cruises, we've been on like four or five cruises. Last year we all went to Jamaica. When we go, she makes sure we get the best of everything and she pays for it all. When she's blessed, she blesses us. That's just the type of person she is. I love it here.

KEY LIME CAKE AT THE BUSY BEE

CAROL JIMENEZ, SEARS FINE FOOD, SAN FRANCISCO, CALIFORNIA

Carol Jimenez

Sears Fine Food | San Francisco, California

My first job was at Manning's. It was a cafeteria-style restaurant (they were all over San Francisco). We used to wear the big puffy handkerchiefs. When I was sixteen, I worked at the Tic-Toc Drive-in. Later, I did office work for about two years, but I didn't like it because it was so confining. I like talking to people and I didn't want somebody trying to shush me in the office. I also worked at a bank and that was a good experience, but they didn't pay any money.

Waitressing keeps your mind really sharp. Because when you go and use the computer, it's doing the work for you. You go up to the computer and think, "Oh, God. What did they have?" When you're calling in an order to the cooks, you have to remember the order. It's do or die.

LAVERNE PHILLIPS, SEVEN SEAS, SAUSALITO, CALIFORNIA. COURTESY OF LAVERNE PHILLIPS.

Even though I'm older, I like to stay active, but I went roller-skating with my great-grandchildren and I broke my thumb and four bones in my arm. I still waitress, but the pain at work gets really bad sometimes. Mostly when it's cold. I just take aspirin and keep going.

Waitressing is not easy, but you do it because you like it. There are a lot of women who have waited tables at some time in their lives, and no matter who does it, even if they don't stay with it, waitressing leaves an impact. You never forget it. I think that most gals who have worked in the industry and made it their life feel that if you took this job away from them it would be the end of their livelihood, because this is different than working in an office or a department store. This is real interaction. I thought about retiring but I just couldn't give it up.

Laverne Phillips

Seven Seas | Sausalito, California

I was born and raised in San Francisco. My mom and I walked across the Golden Gate Bridge the day it opened. I started working when I was in the ninth grade. It was around 1932. I worked with my mother. I think it was called the Canary Den. The meals were fifty cents. They gave my mom a job and she had to be there at four or five o'clock in the morning. Christ, it was a mafia joint [laughing]! She waited on longshoremen too. They were eating roast beef, raviolis, heavy stuff like that, because they had been working since two in the morning. There was a big room in the back and she kept saying, "I think I recognize some of those people and they'd say, 'Oh, never mind that, never mind that, just do your work.'" And then we found out it was mafia because there was a dead body in the back where the cars were parked. It was in the newspapers.

It was hard when I started waitressing. I was a bus girl at Jean Compton's restaurant. It was a cafeteria. I was so short. I couldn't reach the window to get the food out, so I had to step on a box and call the order in. That got a little old. Everybody would laugh like hell at me and say, "Come here, let me show you what this kid's doin'."

That was so long ago. Now I can't imagine having a hard time waitressing. My last job at the Seven Seas restaurant I had seventeen tables—no problem. I like doing what I can to make my customers happy. At the Seven Seas, we didn't have an oil-and-vinegar dressing. We had thousand island, ranch, blue cheese . . . so if a customer asked for an oil-and-vinegar dressing, instead of just giving them the oil and vinegar on the side, I'd ask them, "Are you in a hurry? If you're not in a hurry, I'll make you a dressing." I'd go in the

kitchen and mix up the garlic, oil, and vinegar, I'd break it all up, chop up the onions, toss it. And then take it out and serve it. I fixed it like I would at home. And they'd say, "My God, this is delicious." I had one chef say, "Hey Grandma. Make me one of your dressings." Honest to God, I'm not kidding. So on my days off, people would come in and say, "We want to have that dressing that that older lady fixed for us." And the cooks didn't know how to make it. They were coming unglued!

This is a tough business and you have to stand up for yourself. At the Seven Seas I was waiting on this large round table. They ate a ton of food. They each had a dozen oysters, and then they shared a whole crab, and a combination dinner, with a filet, lobster, and a bottle of wine. The whole time I waited on them I had a funny feeling. So, I said to the other waitress, "Betty, keep an eye on them for me, if you see them going anywhere, let me know." I just had a feeling. So I went to go pick up an order and came out of the kitchen and looked over and they were gone. I said, "Betty! Where'd they go?" She said, "I don't know. I didn't even see them leave." So I ran out the door. And I grabbed a bottle of ketchup on the way. I saw them running across the street and said, "You sons of bitches! Damn you!" And I threw that goddamned bottle and hit one in the head and said "OH MY GOD, I HIT HIM!" I ran like hell back into the restaurant. Anyway, the cops got 'em. Oh, but it scared the hell out of me. I was sure they were going to come back after me.

The Waitressing Stigma

In the 1990s, the television game show *The Family Feud* asked the question, "What occupation would you least like your wife to have?" The number one answer was waitress. Even today, waitressing remains one of the least desired jobs and is rarely taken seriously as a profession. For many, it's a job of last resort—something to fall back on if life doesn't work out as planned. Some even consider it a shameful profession. In Leon Elder and Lin Rolens's book *Waitress: America's Unsung Heroine,* some waitresses refused to be interviewed. Linda Grim, a former waitress, said, "At first, I was reluctant to appear in this book. . . . For one thing, my husband thinks I work in a bank."

It's not surprising that the job carries a negative connotation. Take the word "lifer," for example. It literally means a prisoner serving a life sentence. When applied to a waitress, it suggests a life full of struggle, physical labor, and destitution. Despite its negative associations, career waitresses use the term to make a distinction between themselves and other waitresses. Like many groups of stereotyped people, they have taken a negative label and used it themselves, effectively taking the power out of the word. When asked about being called a "lifer," Sondra Dudley of the Butter Cream Bakery & Diner in Napa, California, said, "A lifer? That's what I am. And proud of it!"

People assume lifers are uneducated and consequently don't have any other career options. But there are many waitresses who are college educated. Paula Hazzouri, a waitress at the Buena Vista Cafe in San Francisco, has a degree from Boston University. She said, "My parents were *so* embarrassed that I waitressed my entire life. This is not what I was supposed to do."

Joyce Widmann, a feisty New Jersey waitress, also defended her choice to wait tables. She said, "I don't like it when people say, 'Oh, she's just a waitress.' As though it's not a real job. I've done other 'real' jobs. I have my real estate license, but I prefer to do this."

Hollywood also perpetuates the image of the sad, downtrodden waitress. Since the 1920s, waitresses have been portrayed in cinema as low-class women with loose morals who will turn to prostitution or homicide to get what they want. If she's not dangerous, then she's usually a single, uneducated woman. The image of the struggling waitress is so prevalent in our minds, when we see her in a film her back story is already complete. In the 1990 film *White Palace,* Susan Sarandon works in a hamburger restaurant and refers to herself as a "waitress" only when she puts herself down. But when she's trying to fit in at an upper class party with her new boyfriend, when asked about her job, she answers, "I'm in uh . . . food preparation."

JOYCE WIDMANN, CRYSTAL DINER, LAWRENCEVILLE, NEW JERSEY

Picking up plates with half-eaten food has its downside. Kathleen Woody, a waitress at Ryan's in Florence, Alabama, admits that touching dirty dishware is something she'd rather not do. She said, "The silverware soaking area makes me feel like I should have been an orthodontist because I always feel like I'm in someone's mouth."

Cleaning up after strangers is similar to being a maid, a nanny, or a nurse. Although these jobs are essential, they are devalued.

Class becomes a critical factor when people are paying for service because it automatically puts the recipient in a position of power. Regardless of how socially conscious someone is, there is something deep in the human psyche that regards service work as less meaningful, as unimportant, and almost taken for granted. Linda Exeler of Erlanger, Kentucky, said, "Some people look down on waitresses. They feel like they're better than us. [They say] 'Get me this or get me that!' It's too bad that they're like that, because, you know, I have no problem getting anything. Actually, I'll walk an extra hundred miles for 'em if I had to. That's how much I enjoy it."

The stereotype that frustrates most servers is that they are not intelligent. "People think we're stupid," said Wilma Mobbs of Sears Fine Food in San Francisco. "I didn't have a college education. I could have gotten a degree if I wanted one, but I happened to like waitressing so I stayed with it." At the Seville Diner, a customer told Sammi DeAngelis, "You're just doing this because you are not smart enough to do anything else." Sammi said, "Excuse me? I have a degree, I could be teaching. I've done public relations and business management. . . . I tell you what, if you can do my job for an hour, this money is yours." After an hour, the customer said, "I've been watching you and you know that last table was really a handful. Maybe I couldn't do your job." Sammi said, "'Really? What part of it didn't you get: the public relations, the psychology, the physical?' I wasn't nasty, but she respected my honesty. Now she's one of my regular customers, she likes to sit with me so she can watch me work."

Angel Stam, a waitress at Sears Fine Food, said, "About 30 percent of our customers have an attitude with servers. Even today, I heard one of our servers get yelled at by a customer for no reason. I tell my trainees, 'Don't take flack from customers. They're not better than you.'"

LINDA EXELER, COLONIAL COTTAGE, ERLANGER, KENTUCKY

Being a Servant

In the Victorian tradition, servants were trained to be so discreet as to almost be invisible. In the eighteenth century the English elite used dumbwaiters so the privileged could speak freely without the irritating presence of a servant. When meals were hand delivered, the best servants could enter and leave a room without anyone noticing. Keeping servants invisible is a powerful psychological tool to keep them in their place.

Fred Harvey created America's version of the ideal servant. He was an ambitious entrepreneur from England who started the first restaurant chain in America. His Harvey Houses lined the Santa Fe Railway in the late 1800s. When the trains pulled in for a quick stop, riders could get a gourmet meal at a reasonable price. Compared to the roadside slop dished out of trailers in most small western towns at the time, eating at a Harvey House was like attending a royal feast.

Harvey's servers were not to be called waitresses. He thought that was a degrading term. Instead, they were "Harvey Girls." Fred Harvey recruited "attractive, young women of good moral character." He found most of his waitresses in the Midwest and brought them out West to serve in his restaurants, because he thought most of the women already living in the West at that time were too adventurous and independent to be Harvey Girls. He searched for "good girls" who were naive and sheltered. Many grew up in rural communities and were predominately white, with the exception of a small group of Mexican and Native American women who worked in the Harvey Houses in the Southwest.

The Harvey Girls became known as "the women who opened up the West." They were the epitome of the feminized ideal: obedient, depersonalized, and controlled with machine-like efficiency. They served fifteen million meals a year and could deliver a trainload of people a five-course meal in less than a half an hour. Fred Harvey controlled their housing, clothing, makeup, and attitude in an almost fetishistic manner. Everything had to be sanitized, not only the clothes they wore but also their lifestyle and even their thoughts. Strict, businesslike formalities were enforced on their waiting style and on their living conditions. If they had a stain on their uniform it had to be changed immediately. Harvey Girls lived on the premises and were told when to go to bed, what jewelry they could wear, and who they were allowed to date. They were not permitted to display any variation in style or personality, and they were dressed to look like domestic maids. In the *Leavenworth Times* in 1905, Elbert Hubbard wrote, "The girls at a Fred Harvey place never look dowdy, frowsy, tired, slipshod or overworked. They are expecting you—clean collars, clean aprons, hands and faces washed, nails manicured—there they are, bright fresh healthy and expectant."

From Harvey Girl to Hasher

Harvey Girls were the antithesis of diner waitresses, who were also known as "hashers" (a term that became popular in the 1930s). "Hasher" not only described waitresses who worked in hash houses or diners; it also described her character, which was usually a woman who was free with her speech and attitude. In 1937, the *Literary Digest* published an article titled, "No Hashers: Waitresses Now Must Have Tact and Charm." The *Digest* said that a diner waitress was "an untidy, uneven-tempered, unpredictable creature."

Charlotte Solbern and Fern Osborn are sisters who worked as Harvey Girls at the Grand Canyon Caverns in the 1960s. They were raised with five other sisters in Nelson, Arizona, an old mining town near Route 66. Their mother watered the steam trains at the Seligman, Arizona, Harvey House station. The Grand Canyon Caverns Harvey House was the prime stopping point for tourists traveling to visit the Grand Canyon. It was a good place for waitresses to make money but working for Fred Harvey involved great personal sacrifice. Charlotte remembered how strict the Caverns were: "You couldn't chew gum, you couldn't smoke, you had to be real neat, and you had to wear a starched uniform, black dresses, black nylon stockings, and white pinafores. Oh I hated them things!"

Even though Charlotte and Fern worked at the Harvey House in the 1960s, the uniform was not so different from the ones Fred Harvey had introduced in 1883. Standing behind the bar in her proper

MURAL OF HARVEY GIRLS BY ALICE KAY, SELIGMAN, ARIZONA

(RIGHT) FERN OSBORN AS A HARVEY GIRL. COURTESY OF FERNANDA OSBORN.

RENEE DONATI, HARRY'S PLAZA CAFE, SANTA
BARBARA, CALIFORNIA

the hassle of fighting off uninvited sexual advances from men. She said, "I would get hotel room keys placed underneath the check. I never understood why I was treated this way."

Since the turn of the twentieth century, waitresses have been burdened with the reputation of having loose morals. It's assumed that they use their sexuality to increase their tips. Although most of the waitresses interviewed denied flirting for tips, still many felt they were treated like "whores" and had to establish clear boundaries. Waitresses reported being pinched, grabbed, hassled, and groped at their most vulnerable times—while carrying trays and glasses. Renee Donati, a waitress at Harry's Plaza Cafe in Santa Barbara, said, "When one customer couldn't keep his hands to himself, I took that coffee pot and poured the coffee right in his lap."

Some men just flat-out propositioned their waitress as though she were a prostitute. Maria Terry, a waitress in Lexington, Kentucky, at the Churchill Downs racetrack said, "One guy came in and asked me, 'How much?' I said, 'How much for what?' He said, '$25, $50?' Once I realized what he was asking for, I couldn't believe it!" Waitresses thought that as they aged, the flagrant solicitations would stop, but they didn't. Rachel DeCarlo from Sittons North Hollywood Diner was asked out well into her seventies.

The assumption that waitresses are sexually available isn't a recent one. In the early twentieth century when police arrested prostitutes and asked about their profession, many lied and said they were waitresses to explain the cash they were holding. In the book *Dishing It Out: Power and Resistance among Waitresses in a New Jersey Restaurant,* Greta Foff Paules references James West's book *Plainville*

uniform and polished shoes, Fern wore her hair pinned back and bound up in a suffocating hair net, her spirit tamed and put under wraps, disinfected and safely managed in mesh, nylon, and starch.

During the heyday at the Caverns, Fern worked double shifts. To save on driving time and gas she lived on the property designated for the staff. "They called it 'Tin City'" she said, "but they were really shacks." One year she moved a trailer up there. She would get three free meals, and they charged her only nine and a half cents a day, utilities included.

Despite the living conditions and the strict rules, Fern stayed because she made good money. At the Caverns she could count on making $150 on the morning shift, and if she worked in the cocktail lounge at night she made $250 in tips. But with the money came

U.S.A., written in 1945. He writes, "A girl who left her hometown to become a waitress in the regional metropolis was generally assumed to have become a prostitute also." In Dorothy Sue Cobble's book, *Dishing It Out: Waitresses and Their Unions in the Twentieth Century*, an Illinois waitress said people think "a waitress is one step ahead of a hussy and losing ground fast."

Needless to say, being a waitress is fundamentally different from being a prostitute, but some similarities might help to explain why they are treated in the same way. Working in a cash-for-services job echoes the idea of selling services for money, and for many waitresses they are selling not only food but also companionship and comfort. Some waitresses admitted that the act of taking

cash rather than being paid with a check initially made them feel uncomfortable. In almost every job, other than those in the service industry, cash is never immediately given. Most workers have to wait two weeks to get paid. Although waitresses do get paychecks, the bulk of their income is made in tips. In American society, quick cash usually denotes illegal activity such as drug dealing, prostitution, or working under the table to avoid paying taxes, all of which have a hint of underhandedness.

Another reason waitresses are stigmatized is that people assume they use their sexuality to make larger tips. Since eating is one of the most intimate acts we do in public, the restaurant environment is rife with sexual undertones. It all starts with desire: "I want" "Can I have" "I'll take." Wearing makeup and jewelry, doing her hair, nails, or prettying herself up in any way—even if she's doing it only for herself—is subconsciously read as a sexual advance or a flirtation. Through no fault of their own, even the most conservative waitresses become fetishized and feed the hetero-male fantasy of being serviced by women—if not sexually, than at the very least, maternally. The most innocent gestures become sexualized: prolonged eye contact, looking over her shoulder to check on a table, stuffing cash into her hip-hugging apron, holding her writing pad at breast level, bending over to pick up glassware.

Another parallel between waitresses and prostitutes is that waitresses are paid for their time and companionship. One waitress freely called herself a "counter whore," because she loved to work the counter. Of course she used the word "whore" not for its literal meaning but a figurative one. Customers pay waitresses to service them and if they sit too long in their station, waitresses get irritated because they could be making money off of a new table. Mindful customers will leave extra money for their waitress if they stayed too long. Although there are many professions where people are paid for their time, a waitress's time is spent very differently from, say, a lawyer who bills by the minute for reading law briefs; a waitress, however, is paid to use her kindness and personality to supply comfort. It's a blurry line that gets crossed in the minds of not only men but also women.

Edie Schrage's mother died before she could find the courage to tell her about her waitressing career. "I was afraid to tell my mom that I was a waitress because she thought all waitresses were trashy people and alcoholics," she said. "We would be out in public and my mom would point to a woman and say, 'I'll bet she's a waitress.' I'd say, 'How do you know?' She'd answer, 'Look at all that makeup and those clothes!'"

Dressing the Part

Whether her sexuality is exaggerated or suppressed, uniforms put waitresses psychologically in the mode of service. Employees in the same uniform sends a message that they will provide the same outstanding service. In the book *The Service Encounter: Managing Employee/Customer Interaction in Service Businesses*, Barry Blackman says that the uniform acts as a tool to subordinate workers, shedding them of personal freedom, and ultimately putting them under the control of their employers.

Before the 1920s most waitresses dressed in prim, buttoned-up black-and-white uniforms. From the 1920s to the 1960s the style shifted from the Fred Harvey matronly look complete with hairnets and opaque black stockings to sexually suggestive fetish wear with short hip-hugging skirts, fitted bust-revealing tops, and knee-high leather go-go boots. "The things they made us wear back then," Kathleen remembers. "It was almost embarrassing to go to work." In the 1960s Laverne didn't even wear pants at the Velvet Turtle. She worked in ruffled panties.

Most waitresses preferred functional uniforms that were loose and comfortable with large pockets to carry necessary work items such as pads, pens, and extra silverware. Over the last fifty years waitress unions have banded together to speak out against the ruffled panties and high heels they were forced to wear. Attention-grabbing, sexed-up outfits were no longer cute. They were considered offensive and insulting to women. Although there are still some restaurants that dress waitresses as sex objects, they stand out as the exception.

Being in Charge

Despite the stigma associated with the job, most lifers have found their place in the industry and feel proud rather than ashamed of their profession. In 1947 the sociologist William Foote Whyte wrote about how waitresses claim their territory and take control at the table: "The skilled waitress tackles the customer with confidence and without hesitation. For example, she may find that a new customer has seated himself before she could clear off the dirty dishes and change the cloth. He is now leaning on the table studying the menu. She greets him, says, 'May I change the cover please?' and, without waiting for an answer, takes his menu away from him so that he moves back from the table and she goes about her work. The relationship is handled politely but firmly, and there is never any question as to who is in charge."

Susan Thurmond of Reno, Nevada, agreed. "I couldn't be any further from feeling like a servant. At work, there's nothing I can't handle. I'm in control." And for the customers who give her a hard time, she said with a serious look on her face, "I'm the one bringing your food. How long do you want it to take?"

Claiming their authority and taking control allows veteran waitresses to redefine the role of being a servant. It's an understated, graceful defiance that is not conscious on her part. She doesn't have to fight for something that she knows she already has. Society doesn't have to recognize or acknowledge her contribution when she leaves work with cash in hand, financially stable, emotionally secure, and fulfilled by who she is and what she does. These women don't care if people look down on them for being "just a waitress." Perhaps it's the result of living long enough to know what's really important in life. Ronnie Bello, who waitressed at the Boulevard Diner in Worcester, Massachusetts, said, "I am not ashamed to be a waitress. I can walk with judges and lawyers, I can fit in with anyone because I know what I do and I'm no phony. This is me. I'm a good waitress, I love people and that's my attitude and if you don't like me for that, that's your problem. I'm not a snob."

RONNIE BELLO, BOULEVARD DINER, WORCESTER, MASSACHUSETTS

Ronnie Bello

Boulevard Diner | Worcester, Massachusetts

I started waitressing for the Blake brothers at Friendly's—they gave the finest training there. In the 1970s I worked at the Almaraco. It was one of the well-known restaurants in Worcester where the celebrities would come to eat. I served Tony Bennett, Bette Midler, Liza Minnelli, Margaret Whiting, Julius La Rosa, and Frankie Vincent, who played in *The Sopranos* (he looked exactly the same then). I stayed there for about fifteen years, it was a wonderful place to work and an experience I will never forget.

I was raised to be a hard worker. My mom and my dad worked hard. I guess you could say that waitressing is a tough job, but to me, this isn't hard and I don't think I'd ever be happy sitting behind a desk. I'm a mover. I don't like sitting still.

Waitressing was the perfect job to raise my kids because it was mother's hours and I could always be home in time to cook a meal for my children when they got home from school. It also provided me with the money I needed to raise my children and my three grandchildren, who all went to private school—on a waitress's salary. Yes, I sometimes worked extra hours to give them everything they needed, but it was worth it.

I don't think the kids today have the stuff that the older girls have. And I think things are handed to them too easily, and I don't think they really know what work is. They don't want to be here. I used to train the kids at the Almaraco and I'd tell them, "If you don't want to be here, find something you like. I don't care if you drive a taxicab or clean a sewer. I don't care what you do, but you be happy."

You have to think, what are your rewards? For me it's more important to see that I've done something with my heart for somebody, instead of just thinking of myself, which is what I think is wrong with this whole world. I get customers coming in here bitching over nothing and I say to them, "You should come with me to the hospital where I volunteer and see children who are burnt all over their bodies; some have no arms or fingers. One girl has no eyes and yet she's smiling everyday. You come in here and you have everything and *you're* bitching?" I tell them, "Spend a little time with someone, do a little something for somebody else and you won't be so bitchy." You find it's the ones with the most that complain the most. Isn't that the way?

I've accomplished a lot in my life. And maybe not moneywise to some people, but I've accomplished a lot of humanity things that mean something to me anyway. You know to someone else it's a whole different ballgame. If you want the new house, the new car, and the diamonds then, no, I haven't succeeded. But I can turn around and say that I've brought up three beautiful children and then three beautiful grandchildren and they're all healthy and they've had their problems, but they're great. That's my wealth.

FERN OSBORN, COPPER CART, SELIGMAN, ARIZONA

Fern Osborn
Copper Cart | Seligman, Arizona

I've worked all of my life. I was raised in Nelson, Arizona, and I started waitressing when I was eleven years old, it was on a reservation at the Kamacha Cafe in Peach Springs.

I was a good waitress because I love people. I used to have restaurant owners come from Las Vegas and ask me to go back with them to wait tables because I was fast. Back then we didn't have trays or little carts to put your dirty dishes in. We had to carry everything. It was important that you never came back to the kitchen empty-handed. You always picked up dirty dishes on the way. You *never* walked by a dirty table and said, "I can go back." Never. You were wasting time.

I've worn my hair like this since 1962. I tease my hair and I use Stiff Stuff from WalMart to keep it up there. My daughter says, "Mother, you need to get rid of that hairdo." And I say, "I'm known for my hair!" I've had people come and take pictures of me and do paintings, but it wasn't because of me, it was because of this [points to her hair]. Kids will come in and say, "Your hair is funny." And their parents would get embarrassed and I say, "No, that's okay, I'm used to it." I cut my hair once and I just cried. I'll never do that again. I know it's old fashioned, but it's me. And this is nothing. It used to be much higher. Me and my sister Charlotte wore our hair so high, we couldn't get into our vehicles [laughing]! We needed a double sunroof just to fit our hair!

The only thing I wanted to do other than waitress was that I wanted to take care of old people. I invite them over to my house. A lot of them are poor and their families don't want nothing to do with them. When people ask, "Why do you bring these people into your house?" I say, "Because nobody wants them and someday we might be like that and we'll wish someone cared." I just see them walking around and they look lost. I drive up and down the streets and I tell them, "I'm having a big shindig at my house, come on over." I put on some music and I get them up to dance and they start dancing and we just have a great time. They tell me, "You're such a wonderful hostess." I hug them and I kiss them. I have these two old cowboys that come over for Thanksgiving and Christmas and my sister said, "Fern, if you invite those cowboys we're not coming because they smell so bad." I say, "What are you going to do just sit there and smell them? Regardless of what they smell like they're still human." I've always said if I ever won the lottery I would build a home here for them. I love my old people. I really do.

FERN (IN RED) AND HER SISTER CHARLOTTE (IN WHITE). THEIR HAIR IS REAL. COURTESY OF FERNANDA OSBORN.

Angel Stam

Sears Fine Food | San Francisco, California

I'm the oldest one here. I train most of the new servers. A lot of them think I'm too bossy. I don't want to be nobody's boss. I just want you to do the perfect job. So I don't have to hear it from the manager. Either I'm going to do it perfect or I won't do it at all. But I tell them, "If you want to learn, you've gotta do it my way."

I can carry seven to eight plates on one arm at a time and a couple in the other hand. But now as I'm getting older, it's very challenging. My shoulder's killing me—it's like carpal tunnel of the shoulder. But I used to carry that way all time. My customers would be so impressed. For instance, if I had a party of ten people, I'd carry it all there. I try and teach the younger servers how to carry, but a lot of them are afraid. They think they're going to drop the plates.

There are some people who appreciate what we do, but a lot of them look down their nose at you because you're a server. I'll go out and meet a new friend or neighbor and they ask, "What do you do for a living?" I say, "I'm a waitress." And they say, "Oh, a waitress, interesting [disapproving tone]." Sometimes I get defensive and say, "You might work in an office, but I probably make twice more than you, so don't even go there."

I deal with hundreds of people all day long and I don't take any BS from anybody. If somebody is being nasty with me, I will confront them. And if I did something wrong, I don't mind saying, "I'm sorry, I made a mistake." But for people to be nasty for no reason doesn't make sense. If some of my customers are mean, I say, "You know what, you better go find another waitress or another restaurant because I've had it with you." They've had a bad day? So what. That's not my fault. If I did something wrong then I can understand, but to just constantly complain and run you back and forth. After three or four times of this, you get tired. Then they get mad and say, "Well, you're my server." And I say, "Listen. You're not my only customer. I have twenty more customers." I don't let people step on me because then I'm upset for no reason. I'm not the type to hold a grudge. I just tell them how I feel and move on.

My regulars are great. After so many years, they become your friends. We exchange birthday gifts and everything. We have these regulars we call the Bingo Boys. They've taken us [and the other waitress, Carol] out to play bingo with them, and we've gone with them to the Indian casino a couple of times. They love it when we come.

Sears was closed temporarily and the customers took it pretty hard. They didn't know if we were ever going to reopen. Everybody was crying and exchanging phone numbers. They all gave us business cards and said, "Whenever you need something, call us." It was amazing.

T.I.P.S. To Insure Prompt Service

The reward for managing chaos is the tip. Although most career waitresses are not motivated entirely by money, it does encourage them to do their best. Faye Blackwell of the Trio Restaurant in Washington, D.C., said, "I think tipping is the only way this business will ever work. It's good for the customer and for the waitress. This job is so stressful, most people wouldn't put up with the rudeness of some customers if it weren't for the tips."

Most historians agree that tipping started in English coffee houses in the early seventeenth century. Customers put money in boxes labeled "TIPS," an acronym meaning "To Insure Prompt Service." The word "tip" is derived from the Latin word *stips*, meaning "gift." Tipping has become a standard social practice in the United States and is not only expected but in some restaurants required. Although it's regularly practiced today, in the early twentieth century the tipping system was challenged and considered un-American. From 1905–19, the Anti-tipping Society successfully lobbied to abolish tipping in seven states. By 1919, however, the law was repealed and labeled unconstitutional.

The Bureau of Labor Statistics reports that servers average about ten dollars an hour, but career waitresses are not the destitute laborers society labels them. Despite the interviewees who had money problems due to medical bills or unforeseen circumstances, most said they were averaging $20 to $30 an hour, making waitressing one of the more lucrative jobs that requires no formal education.

In the 1920 book *The Woman Who Waits*, author Frances Donovan estimated that 40 percent of the waitresses she studied were divorced. Most of the waitresses I interviewed were divorced and preferred to stay single, as their salary allowed them to be self-sufficient. Many of the married women were the primary wage earners in their family. Some supported their husbands in school; others admitted that their ex-husbands were drinkers and gamblers and didn't contribute when it came to taking care of the family. The first husband of Fern Osborn of Seligman, Arizona, worked at the Nelson Chemical Lime Plant. She said, "He made about $13–$14 an hour. But with my tips, I made more money. I paid my trailer payments, my car payments. . . . It was like I really didn't even need him."

Waitresses' hours are often the opposite of their husbands' nine-to-five schedules, which can cause problems in the relationship. Carol Jimenez's husband worked a regular job during the week and he didn't like that she worked on weekends. But she loved working the counter at Sears Fine Food in downtown San Francisco, *especially* on the weekend. Her favorite regulars came in every Saturday morning and it was the busiest time of the week, so she made excellent money. When her husband pressured her with an ultimatum about her job, they eventually divorced. She remembered, "When I had to work weekends, we were not happy campers. That's what did it."

Waitressing may not have been great for marriages, but it was a good job to raise children. Rachel DeCarlo's son Harold liked having a mother as a waitress. He said, "My mom worked in a Jewish deli and I'd get the best sandwiches to take to school. All the other kids had skimpy bologna sandwiches made with air bread, or Wonder Bread, whatever that stuff was that you could squeeze into a ball. I had exotic breads like black bread and marble rye and a pile of five or six slices of ham. There was no comparison. Also, I got my work ethic from watching my mom. She was a hard worker and she was good at what she did. When we got home at night I would rub her calves and her feet and I'd polish her work shoes for the next day."

"My kids never wanted for anything," said Joyce Widmann of Lawrenceville, New Jersey. "They all went to private schools and then on to college. When people come in here wearing business suits and have a snobby attitude and look down on me because I'm a waitress, I think, I'll bet I make more money than you." Wilma Mobbs said, "At Sears Fine Food, we had lines out the door and around the corner. I was making $800–$900 a week. And this was in the 1970s and 80s. I was making more money than most women period at that time."

Even women with college degrees chose waitressing because of the money that could be made. Paula Hazzouri of San Francisco, whose degree is from Boston University, said, "I studied German literature and art history. I could have gotten a job in a museum, but waitressing afforded me more freedom and actually I made more money." Women without college degrees found that waitressing paid more than being a secretary or working in a department store or factory. Georgina Moore of Reno, Nevada, took a two-month leave of absence to work as a secretary, but she was back to wait-

RACHEL DECARLO AND
HER SON HAROLD

ressing after only a month. She said, "I figured after my gas, lunch, and my clothing that I had to buy (because here at the Gold 'n Silver they furnish you with uniforms), I was probably making about $3 an hour as opposed to $25–30 an hour waitressing. And that's after taxes, after my uniform, I eat here for free . . . so there's a big difference. I couldn't give this up."

Although many waitresses say that they would rather have someone treat them with respect and leave an average size tip than treat them badly and leave a large tip, walking out with a pocketful of dollar bills at the end of the day always makes them feel better. To some waitresses making money becomes a game. Susan Thurmond of Henderson, Nevada, said, "It was a thrill to see how much I could make each day." Dolores Jeanpierre, a waitress in Alameda, California, has seniority at Ole's Waffle Shop, so she's able to work the most lucrative shifts. On Fridays she can make $250–$300 in tips, plus $8 an hour in wages.

Despite the money that can be made, not all waitresses earn a good living. In fact, many servers make less because they haven't paid their dues. It takes decades of experience and work in the same restaurant to build a large, regular clientele who tip better than the average customer. Waitresses who serve both regulars and tourists immediately notice the difference between the tips. The distinction is not only in the amount but also in the way the money is given. A regular offers money as a genuine sign of appreciation while

PAULA HAZZOURI, BUENA VISTA CAFE, SAN FRANCISCO, CALIFORNIA

some tourists leave money out of obligation. This is especially true in restaurants that cater to tourists from cultures that don't have a standardized tipping system. Paula serves both locals and tourists at the Buena Vista Cafe in San Francisco. She said, "The tourists are the reason why I don't work weekends. They don't have a clue. They have dinner and then they don't tip. It's awful."

Although tourists tend to tip less, not all regulars start out as good tippers. "Sometime it takes years to start getting good tips," said Kathleen Woody of Florence, Alabama. "This one customer, boy, was he a tall drink of water. He'd leave only twenty-five cents and then once I got to know him and we got to talking . . . well, I'm up to five bucks now. So you can increase your tip flow. You have to work at it, but it comes."

Without the tipping system, waitresses would starve, as their money does not come from their employers. In most states, waitresses don't make even the minimum wage but instead earn a special, lower wage for servers. For example, in Arizona the minimum wage is $6.90 an hour, but the wage for waitresses is only $2.75. And that was just increased from $2.15 in 2006.

The hourly wage varies from state to state. In southern Nevada, less than fifty miles away from Arizona, waitresses do much better financially. By the time Virginia Brandon retired from the Rainbow in Henderson, Nevada, she was making about $8 an hour. But like most waitresses, she started out making $2 an hour and worked her way up. She remembered, "I was talking to this customer about money and I told him I make about $7 an hour and he said, 'Wow!

That's really good for a waitress.' And I said, 'Well damn, I've been working here twenty-five years." Virginia moved to Nevada specifically for the higher wages and because there were more union restaurant jobs. She said, "Being in a union house makes all the difference. It gives the workers even more control. If the restaurant is empty at 9:00 p.m. and our shift isn't over until 11, the manager can't send us home. We make every dollar coming to us."

Southern Nevada has some of the best earning opportunities for waitresses in the United States. They are paid a fair living wage along with health and retirement benefits. The culinary union is a powerful influence that creates a competitive environment which benefits restaurant workers. To compete with union houses, non-union restaurants have to offer similar benefits. Most waitresses in other U.S. states have to work an office job at some time during their career to have medical insurance for their family. In Nevada, however, especially in the Vegas area, waitresses are offered a complete health care (medical/dental/vision) and retirement package. Susan said, "Here, waitressing is as good as going to school and getting your degree and being somebody. Just look at our bank accounts."

Waitresses don't have to live in Nevada to reap special benefits from their employers. Geri Spinelli started working at the Melrose Diner in Philadelphia when she was a teenager. She said, "This is the best place to work. We average $6.10 an hour when the minimum wage for waitresses is about $2.38. We have a good health plan and hospitalization. We get a good salary, plus tips, a Christmas bonus and paid vacations. I'll get three weeks of paid vacation this year. It's great."

MELROSE DINER, PHILADELPHIA, PENNSYLVANIA

Although some waitresses said their employers offered health and retirement benefits, the majority didn't receive anything. Less than 20 percent had paid vacations. One waitress said, "After you work someplace for twenty years, you should be able to take a week off." The waitresses who weren't lucky enough to work in a place that went above and beyond to recognize and respect their workers made do with what they had. Most waitresses are natural-born sales ladies. The more they sell, the more money they make. Rachel Lelchuck of San Francisco could sell cheesecake for breakfast. She said, "If we had fresh cantaloupe, I'd bring a big silver bucket to their table. They looked so good, the customers couldn't resist. I'd sell the whole batch within an hour." Sammi DeAngelis of East Brunswick, New Jersey, agrees. "If you know what you're doing you can make money. I ring over $1000 in sales a night, when most of the waitresses here only ring about $600. I'm known for my sundaes. It's all about presentation. I add sprinkles, a cherry, and a little panache. I've seen girls come to a table with a plain-looking sundae and wonder why they only get a two-dollar tip and I'm getting five. It's not rocket science."

Holidays and birthdays are also good for waitresses with a lot of regular customers. Esther Paul of Gardnerville, Nevada, said, "You would not believe the money my customers leave, especially on my birthday. Every table has at least five dollars on it, and I have ten tables. So when you figure how many times I can turn them in eight hours . . . it adds up."

The tipping system requires that a waitress have an entrepreneurial spirit because ultimately she is responsible for how much she earns. Annie King, a waitress at the Venus Diner in Gibsonia, Pennsylvania, summed it up: "How much money you make is up to you. If you're mean and nasty and don't give people good service—they don't tip you. And I don't blame them. You have to earn it."

Some older waitresses think that the younger, prettier waitresses make better tips, but Susan said that experience brings in the money. "The young ones want to work the counter because they can make good money," she said, "but a lot of them can't handle the pace." When Susan goes to pick up her orders from the kitchen the customers at the counter are so frustrated with their waitress, they throw their hands up in the air. "I ask them, 'What do you need? What can I do for you honey?' So I grab what I can for them while I make it back to my tables. This is how you get call parties. The next time that customer comes in, they ask to sit in my section."

When waitresses complain to Ellen Warren-Seaton, who manages the USA Country Diner in Windsor, New Jersey, about their tips, she says, "Honey, you're talking to the wrong lady. Because I've worked this floor and I know you can make money. If you're not making money it's because you're not doing something right. You're not taking care of your tables or you're hanging out in the back, so you're only going to get a couple of dollars in tips. But if you stay out here in the front and work hard, you're going to go home with money in your pocket."

Restaurants jobs where waitresses make good money are not easy to come by. Servers have to practically die before there is an opening. One place Laverne Phillips of Sausalito, California, worked didn't have a job opening for several years. She remembered, "Those girls would work. They wouldn't even stop to eat, and they never took a vacation, because the money was so good. I barely even went to the bathroom when I was at work. I was like a camel. I could hold it forever."

Some newer restaurants pool tips, which are then averaged out so everybody makes the same amount. Veteran waitresses are adamantly against this practice because they know they can make more than the average server. Virginia said, "Some of those waitresses will wait on ten tables and I'll wait on twenty, and then they want to split the tip? I don't think so."

Waitresses have to be smart about how they handle their taxes. In the 1970s the government suspected that waitresses were not claiming all of their tips, and a large number of them were audited. Virginia remembered, "I really got nailed. When I started we wrote down whatever we wanted, so some of us would claim only $2 a day and there was always that one honest person who would claim $100 a day, so the rest of us got audited one year and I ended up paying . . . oh God, I don't know how much I paid, but they were garnishing

ANNIE KING, VENUS DINER, GIBSONIA, PENNSYLVANIA

my checks. We refused to pay taxes because we considered it a gift from our customers, not income, you know."

To insure they get paid, the IRS calculates the sales waitresses make in each pay period and takes out eight percent. Virginia said, "Our two-week checks went from like $400 to less than $100. But at least we didn't have to worry about getting audited."

The system is far from perfect. Waitresses who work in New Jersey such as Sammi are making only $2.13 an hour. She said, "You'd be amazed how many people think we make the state minimum wage and that our tips are extra. In New Jersey, it's been almost thirteen years since there has been a wage increase for waitresses. New Jersey just raised the minimum wage and we got nothing." One customer said to her, "Well, you're going home with at least what I make. Why should I tip you?" Sammi showed him her paycheck and said, "Here, read it. After making only $2.13 an hour and all of the tax deductions, this check is $47.45. I worked 52.50 hours and I'm taking home $47.45. They go by our gross sales. They don't care what you actually made. In other words, if you come in to have dinner and it was $100 check, they're saying we should have made $15–$18 on that check, if you leave me $5, I'm still paying on $18, regardless." And it's even worse for waitresses who don't work overtime like Sammi. Their two-week paycheck is less than a dollar, and some even get voided checks.

Waitresses who work in coffee shops where people are notorious for not tipping at all are in a bad position because for every customer who doesn't tip, the waitress has to pay out money. At the Gold 'n Silver in Reno, a sign on every table informs customers of this. Georgina said that when she has a chronic stiffer, "We'll make them sit there a half an hour before we take his order. They'll start tipping or they won't come back anymore."

Career waitresses don't like stiffers, but some understand that not everyone can afford to leave 15 percent. When seniors on a fixed income leave only a quarter at the Seven Seas, Laverne said, "Hey, they got their social security check and this was their big day out. If I could have afforded to pick up the check I would have. That's the way I feel about it. I don't see a dollar sign coming in, I see a human being." Despite Laverne's generous nature, one customer gave her no choice but to say something about his poor tipping. "He would bring in twenty people at a time and would leave me a five-dollar tip." She said, "After I got to know him, I said, 'Would you please call and let me know when you're coming?' Because I had to give up two or three of my tables just to wait on him. At first all the man left was five dollars and I thought, oh well, what the heck, I'll let it go, I'll make it up. And then one day he came in and I said, 'Honey, I just can't afford to wait on you this week. I have bills to make.' He said, 'What do you mean?' I said, "The way you tip is what I mean. You spend $200 for dinner and then you leave me $5?" He said, "Well, what is an appropriate tip?" And I said 15 percent, if you like me. If you don't, keep leaving the $5. So after that I always got 15 percent and then another $10 or $20. He was embarrassed, he really didn't know."

Most career waitresses said that money is a small part of the job. In fact, some said they weren't even working for the money—they had inheritances, their husband's pensions, or enough in savings to pay the bills. To them, the money was gravy. Sondra Dudley, a Napa Valley waitress at the Butter Cream Bakery & Diner said, "I don't have to be here. I'm here because I want to be. My husband makes a good living. I don't have to work if I don't want to."

If the American Dream can be summed up as happiness, prosperity, ownership, and free will, who's to say these women aren't living it? Most of the waitresses interviewed said they have a financially stable life, and, more importantly, are happy with their jobs. Despite their reputation for being poor and struggling, career waitresses still enjoy material comforts. At age seventy-seven Esther gets a new sports car every two years. Wilma was able to hire a live-in nanny for her kids, and the house she bought on a waitress's salary is now worth over $750,000. How is this possible when people who make more than waitresses still have much less? They're good at managing their money. The skills waitresses use to prioritize their time serving thirty people during the lunch rush are the same management and organizational tools they apply to their finances. Just as they don't squander precious time at work, they don't throw away their money on unnecessary things. Wilma said, "It's not how much you make, it's how you manage what you make. I've worked right alongside people over the years who throw away their money on expensive vacations and fur coats and they don't have anything today."

When asked about money for retirement, some waitresses said they would have to work for as long as possible, but almost half didn't seem worried about it. They had invested in mutual funds and antiques, or they had their husband's pensions and social security checks. Esther's system seems to work for her. "I've made some good investments for retirement," she said. "I use my salary for my groceries and utilities and I save my tips. I get a hundred-dollar bill and I save it. I've done that for twenty-five years. When I retire, I'll be just fine."

SONDRA DUDLEY, BUTTER
CREAM BAKERY & DINER, NAPA,
CALIFORNIA

(BELOW) WILMA MOBBS AT HOME,
SAN FRANCISCO, CALIFORNIA

WILMA MOBBS, PHOTOGRAPHED AT LORI'S DINER, SAN FRANCISCO, CALIFORNIA

Wilma Mobbs

Sears Fine Food | San Francisco, California

I started when I was eighteen in Arkansas. I took the Greyhound bus to work from Cabot. It was in a little restaurant called Billy Earl's. There was a gas station out front and a few tables in the back. They were open all night. I made fourteen dollars a week. I worked seven days a week from seven at night until seven in the morning. I did everything. I waited tables, I mopped the floor, took the cash. . . . If somebody wanted a hamburger or eggs I had to cook it.

I wanted to be a nurse, but we were poor so I couldn't afford to go to college. You don't go to college to become a waitress, but now there's a lot of people with big educations doing waiter and waitress work because there's more money in it. A lot of my friends at the St. Francis Hotel have degrees, but they make more money waitressing.

When I worked at Sears it was a union restaurant and we didn't rotate sections. My workstation was called the pit. When you're new you've got to take what you can get. As you work up, you get better stations. You're better off if you work up front because the hostess doesn't seat the tables as often in the back; they don't want to walk all the way back there or something. But I always made better money in the pit. I got it after Ruthie retired. She had been there thirty-five to forty years.

I joined the union around 1959. They give you seniority, vacation time, leave of absence, and higher wages. You get your social security, and they negotiate your health and welfare contracts and then that pays into Medicare for you. They're picketing now and if the hotels don't sign that contract soon, that means I'm gonna lose some health and welfare retirement benefits. This is really important to us.

You had to be good to work at Sears. Al, the owner, was very strict to work for. He showed you everything he wanted done and how he wanted it done. He'd give you a chance to make a mistake, but if you kept doin' it you were dead meat. He was strict, but he was a good man. When his kids took it over things went downhill. . . .

They were sweet but they really didn't know what they were doing.

Now that I'm retired, it's not that bad. I have to keep myself active though. I bounce out of bed and run to the gym about five days a week. I show up at around eight o'clock in the morning and I take two classes. I like kickboxing and aerobics (for seniors), and then I lift weights. I want to be healthy. I may not live to be one hundred, but I'm seventy-four now and as long as I'm here I want to be able to do what I want. I volunteer at the rest home, and that is not living. They're just keeping those people alive. I don't want to be bedridden or dependent on anybody. I've never been able to depend on anybody but myself. My husband didn't last long so I've always had to take care of myself and my kids. It would kill me to have to ask for every thing I needed and wanted so I do everything in my power to try and avoid that.

GERI SPINELLI, MELROSE DINER, PHILADELPHIA, PENNSYLVANIA

Geri Spinelli

Melrose Diner | Philadelphia, Pennsylvania

I'm a Philly girl. I was born and raised in South Philadelphia and I've lived here all my life.

I started working the graveyard shift at the Melrose Diner in 1975. I told the manager I didn't have any experience and he said, "You're hired. You start tonight."

They trained me from the bottom up. I worked from eleven o'clock at night to seven o'clock in the morning. It was a good job to have so I could be with my kids. I've done other work over the years, but I really enjoy waitressing the best. I was a restaurant manager for a short time, but I didn't like it. I'd just rather be with the customers instead of taking care of the scheduling and ordering. I got paid more per hour, but once you figure your hours that

you're putting in and at that place, there were no benefits. It was okay, I guess. It's just a title. But I went back to waitressing because I really missed my customers.

I'm a people person. My mom used to say I have the "gift of gab." I never shut up. Office work to me is boring. I cannot sit in an office all closed up with no sunshine. I've done figure work before and it's boring. Your head is in the books and that's it. Somebody else might love it but it's not for me. A lot of people say, "I don't know how you do this job." I'll be sixty-two years old next month. There's not too many of us old ones left.

GERI WITH HER REGULAR CUSTOMER, MELROSE DINER, PHILADELPHIA, PENNSYLVANIA

KATHLEEN WOODY, RYAN'S, FLORENCE, ALABAMA

Kathleen A. S. Woody
Ryan's | Florence, Alabama

I started my waitressing career when I was twelve years old at the T & J Coffee Shop in Redwood City, California. My daddy owned it. It was downtown and there was a lot of action there, so we stayed pretty busy. After school my mom would pick me up and take me to the coffee shop and I'd work for tips. I picked up a lot of coin back then. And it was real silver coin. They don't have silver coin anymore.

Moving from California to Alabama was a slap in the face. I was making a lot more money hourly in California. I came here and started making $2.13 an hour. So if you want to waitress here, you better be good at what you do. Because tipping is a gamble, nobody has to leave you anything.

It was hard picking up money off of a table, because when I did catering I got a paycheck. But it all adds up. And it does get better. We pick up a lot of one-dollar bills so I have a system. I've said that if I had a son, I'd name him George. When I see Abraham, I get excited. Abraham goes to the Visa bill. I roll my quarters, cause they'll add up to $10. The other change I put in the piggy bank so when Christmas comes around I see what's in the piggy bank. If I get ten dollars, that goes into the Kathleen fund. I go on vacation or spend it on whatever I want.

I graduated from high school and I went on to college. I did two years and graduated with my associate of arts degree. I tell my kids, it's my only regret, that I didn't get my bachelor of arts degree. My brother Tom is a doctor. He has a Ph.D. in psychology. He didn't like the restaurant business. He didn't want to work that hard. I guess it is hard work, but it really doesn't seem that way to me.

Customers expect a lot out of you. We call it showtime. You think people aren't watching you, but they watch every little step, so you have to be careful. You have to be on. And you have to think five or six steps ahead. If you have forty people sitting at eight tables and they all think they are the only ones there, sometimes you have to spread yourself a little thin to satisfy everyone. I had a chef tell me once, "Steal with your eyes." If you're in the weeds and that other girl isn't, watch her and see what she's doing differently. There are certain things you need to do to stay ahead of the game. You have to think ahead and watch every table. You might be clearing this one, but your eyes better be watching the other one while you're doing it and you don't stop. You don't have time to stop. You have to know what you're going to do next.

If you're real restaurant people, it's in your blood. But the work ethic is different now. People just don't want to work hard. I hate to say that it's generational, but for the most part that's true. There are some people my age who will say, "No, I won't do it, it's not worth it." I think well since you're *here,* why not show your job performance? Why let it go downhill? You think you're only going to make one dollar off of a table of ten people? Well you've got to give them that four-star service anyway. People think that anyone can do this job until you start working with them and then you see that they can't do this. She can't clear those tables and get the dishes picked up. She's slower than molasses going uphill on a winter day. The quality of service is fading.

The Generation Gap

There are career waitresses and then there are those who are simply waiting—waiting for a "real" career, to graduate from school, or to begin a better life. When asked about the worst part of the job, almost all career waitresses said that it was working with younger servers. "They just don't get it. It's not in their heart," said Esther Paul of Gardnerville, Nevada, who has been waitressing since 1944. "Newcomers walk in and think, this will be easy. I'll make some big

bucks. But you don't make the big bucks when you first start. Your clientele come back because they liked the service. It's like anything else; you have to give to get."

Veteran waitresses were raised in a time when work choices for women were limited to teacher, secretary, waitress, factory worker, or department store clerk. As waitressing paid better than most jobs available to them, they stayed with it and felt grateful they could support their families. In the 1940s, when many of these women started working, the function of a job was to provide financial support, not to fulfill their life's destiny. Today, people search their souls desperately to figure out their life's calling. It's a privileged dilemma that most older waitresses didn't have.

The younger generation has been raised in a world filled with conveniences and inexpensive time-saving gadgets. Yet somehow the more time we save, the less of it we seem to have. In this quest for more, better, and faster, satisfaction is promised but rarely comes. It's hard to fully appreciate modern conveniences when you've always had them. Older waitresses remember what it was like to live without computers, cell phones, microwaves, televisions, and even washing machines.

Many older waitresses are frustrated with the casual nature and lackluster attitudes of younger servers. They say that kids talk on their cell phones while they're working and are not dressed properly for the job. Years ago the rules were more strict: nylons and hairnets were required. "Things have really changed," said Fern Osborn of Seligman, Arizona. "Now you can wear shorts, scuffed shoes, untucked shirts, wet hair. . . . Back in my day, everybody looked nice. Your shoes had to be polished and your clothes were starched. But now people don't care, they just don't care!"

Every generation finds fault with the younger one. Sometimes the whole point of being young is to have fewer responsibilities and to be carefree and naive. But many older waitresses didn't have that luxury. "We struggled a lot more back then, times were different," Esther said. Most of the waitresses I interviewed grew up doing hard physical labor such as farm work: picking cotton, wheat, onions, and tobacco. They lived in rural environments with few

PAT DERMATIS (IN THE MIDDLE), AGE SIXTEEN, SIP 'N BITE, BALTIMORE, MARYLAND. COURTESY OF PAT DERMATIS.

creature comforts. Some of their parents died young because they had little access to doctors. The children had to grow up fast, some taking care of their family financially or working like an adult in the fields. According to Rivers Coleman, a waitress from Mississippi, "Compared to picking cotton, waitressing was easy."

Virginia Brandon's family has three generations of waitresses. At one time all of them worked at the Rainbow in Henderson, Nevada. The Brandons revealed a spectrum of values, conflicts, and attitudes about the job. Virginia, the grandmother, worked the swing shift; her daughter Susan, in her 40s, worked days; Virginia's granddaughter Brit, age eighteen, worked graveyard; and the other granddaughter Nicole, age twenty, filled in a couple of days a week.

Nicole is a strikingly intelligent woman who graduated from high school with a 4.7 GPA in Clark County, Nevada. She is part of a new generation. She doesn't smoke (which is rare in southern Nevada), and she is striving for a professional career in medicine. She falls under the category of waitresses who are waiting for the next chapter in their lives. While working part time at the Rainbow she was enrolled in premed classes at the University of Las Vegas. In an exasperated tone, Nicole said, "This job is stressful. I don't know how my grandma does it. We call her 'the soldier.' One day she cut her foot with a weed whacker and went to work! She's amazing." Although Nicole works overtime to ace her chemistry classes, when it comes to waitressing she can barely stand two shifts a week. "I work as little as possible," she said. But her grandmother works about six

THE BRANDONS—
SUSAN, VIRGINIA,
BRIT, AND NICOLE—
DRESSED FOR WORK

days a week, because she's covering for all the young people who call in sick. Virginia said, "I've never seen so many young kids so sick all the time. The old gals, we never call in sick."

Defiantly, Nicole said that she did not want to be waitressing at sixty-five years old because she doesn't want to struggle her whole life. But her sense of struggling is a world away from her grandmother's experience as a migrant farmer worker. Nicole's mother, Susan, just wants her daughter to have an easier life. It's natural for parents to want their kids to not have to work as hard as they did. But the question becomes, is an educated life really *easier*? Possibly. But the bottom line is no matter who you are, life is full of challenges. Rich, young, educated, poor, it doesn't matter. The ethical dilemmas Nicole might face as a doctor could bear a psychological weight that her mother or grandmother will never experience as waitresses. But the financial rewards an educated life *can* bring (but often times doesn't) keeps our universities filled to capacity with students accumulating a lifetime of debt. Geri Spinelli of Philadelphia, who has waitressed for about forty years, said, "From what I can tell, I don't think an educated life is a better life. I think what's better is the life that you *choose*, not the one that people think you're supposed to have."

Dr. Jeffrey Arnett, author of *Emerging Adulthood: The Winding Road from Late Teens through the Twenties*, says, "The generation now in their twenties is the most affluent generation in American history, so they have high expectations for life. They not only expect to find a job that pays well, but is also enjoyable." Young women are told they can be anybody they want to be, but there's a downside to having unlimited choices. According to ABC News, millions of people aged twenty to twenty-nine are in therapy due to job-related identity issues. It's so widespread that therapists and mental health experts have labeled their struggles as a "quarter-life crisis."

Many of the kids who follow the rules and get an education are finding that once they graduate, starting salaries are not enough to live on. In Corante, an online technology and business journal, Elizabeth Albrycht argues, "My generation was misinformed about the value of our college degrees. $120,000 of your/our money now buys, career-wise, just a hair more than your free high-school diploma used to. As many of my peers now lament, 'A law degree is the new B.A.' We're the best-educated generation in American history, yet the job requirements haven't changed."

Over the last thirty years, increasingly more kids from blue-collar backgrounds have had the opportunity to go to college. In the early 1900s less than 10 percent of the population even had a high school degree. In the 1940s, about 20 percent had a high school degree, and less than 5 percent had a college degree. In 2005, 49 percent of eighteen- and nineteen-year-olds were enrolled in college. Now armed with an expensive piece of gold-embossed paper, a mountain of student loan and credit card debt, if they are fortunate enough to find a job in their field, it usually doesn't even offer health insurance or retirement benefits. And the basic cost of living is comparably much higher then when their parents were starting out.

It's no wonder the younger generation is frustrated and confused. Now dubbed the entitlement generation, they are starting out their lives with a cynical disbelief in the American Dream. Many grew up believing they could be and do anything they wanted, especially girls who were born in the 1970s during the time of "I am woman, hear me roar." Mothers taught their daughters to aim high and get an education so they could have it all: the family, the career, money, independence, and power. Those who were bred to believe they were destined for greatness are now faced with the reality that life is full of detours and broken promises. The possibility of becoming a lifer is incomprehensible to them. Geri sees this firsthand at the Melrose Diner. She said, "The young ones complain, 'My back hurts. My feet hurt.' I say to them, 'What are you going to do when you become my age? You're twenty-two now, I have forty years on you and you're complaining now? How about when you get older?' They say, 'Oh, I won't be doing this.' I say, 'Boy, I hope to God you're not. Good luck.'"

It's not just the physical demands of the work that cripples the younger generation. In a culture where extreme sports are the rage and the gym is filled with people pushing themselves to exhaustion in kickboxing and spinning classes, it's the psychology of work

GERI SPINELLI, MELROSE DINER, PHILADELPHIA, PENNSYLVANIA

that's at stake here. It's the physical labor compounded with the psychological strain of feeling like a servant—or worse, a nobody.

Older waitresses who were raised during the Depression or the Second World War were constantly reminded to conserve and ration their food and resources. Faye Blackwell of Washington, D.C., said, "I never asked for anything when I was coming up because I knew we couldn't afford it. When my children asked for something, I'd say 'How are you going to pay for that?' So they'd cut people's lawns, or babysit. . . . If I saw they were working hard, I'd get it for

them. But today, children are given so much. And they get really expensive stuff. They don't realize how hard money is to earn."

Another major difference older waitresses see in the younger generation is their math skills. In the mid-1980s the Board of Education allowed students to use calculators for standardized tests. This was a clear message to this generation that it's the end product that counts, not the process, which requires critical insight and thought. Older waitresses can see the impact of this at work. One waitress said, "They're so used to computers and calculators, they can't do the math to tally up checks. If the cash register doesn't tell them the change to give to the customer, they can't figure it out. It really slows us down. There will be a line of people waiting to pay."

Since younger servers view the job as temporary, they are focused on the money and not on developing long-term relationships with their customers. This is especially true when it comes to serving their customers' children. During the thirty years Esther worked Sharkey's, she has waited on three generations of the same family. She sees children as a unique bonding opportunity, creating a familial connection that doesn't interest younger waitresses. Esther said, "The younger waitresses complain, 'I don't want to wait on those little brats!' I tell them, 'Well, those little brats are going to be your customers of tomorrow and they'll probably remember you the next time they come in.'" For the waitress who just wants to make money, families with young children are high maintenance. Toddlers take extra time and effort, babies throw food on the floor, and the parents are so distracted they don't eat as quickly and sit at the table for twice as long. Career waitresses watched these kids grow up, and in some cases when they reach their teens, the kids work for them as bussers during their summer breaks. They know that if they're nice to their customers' children, the parents will stay loyal to her for years to come.

Several restaurant managers said that their older waitresses run circles around the younger servers. "The younger ones just can't cut the mustard," said Elaine Reynoldson, an eighty-year-old waitress from Sun City, Arizona. When Virginia sees a young server dragging her feet, she asks, "Can't you walk any faster than that?" She said, "On my shift we're all older, we have one that's 28, one that's 40 and the rest are over 55. Jerry, our boss, thinks we're great. He's tells these young waitresses who can hardly make it through a shift, 'Look at these women, they should be an inspiration to you.' I don't know why it's harder for them. I can't figure it out. The only thing I can think of is that it's not that they can't do it. It's because they don't *want* to do it."

Carol Jimenez of San Francisco agrees. "It takes a different kind of person to do this work," she said with a serious look. "If you don't want to be here, you are going to have a really hard time. The newcomers are kind of considered outsiders. It's hard to train them. Some of these young ones come in fifteen minutes late everyday. I tell 'em, 'I don't want to do your job. Get here on time and do your own job!'"

At the Butter Cream Bakery & Diner Sondra Dudley said the younger ones call in sick at the last minute. "When I tried to pull that when I was young," she said, "Bobby [the owner] would say, 'You're not sick. I'll give you ten minutes to get here.' Over the years Sondra has showed up to work with everything from broken toes to broken ribs. "When I broke my toe," she said, "I just cut out the top of my shoe and went to work. These kids would be off for weeks."

After a lifer puts in her time, her highly sought-after schedule becomes a status symbol. It's where the ranking system among waitresses is the most apparent, because those who are relegated to working the slower shifts make a fraction of the money. At the Rainbow, a younger waitress asked Virginia, "How did you get that day off?" She answered, "Stay here for twenty-five years and you can have it too. The only reason I got this schedule was because the girl who had the shift got cancer, and I bid for it." Brit, who worked at the Rainbow with her grandmother, Virginia, said, "The other workers would joke around and say, 'Hey, why don't you trip your grandma, so we can have some decent shifts?'"

Even though career waitresses tend to have a better attitude about the job, age does not determine how well a waitress performs. Some older waitresses are notoriously bitter and will complain to anyone who will listen. Sammi DeAngelis of East Brunswick, New Jersey, said, "I'd like to strangle this older waitress I work with. She has no professional courtesy. She never restocks her station, so when she leaves there's no syrup, creamers or even coffee. *Hello?* It's a diner. She does it all the time and no one says a word. It drives me crazy."

Despite all the problems with the newcomers, older waitresses admitted there are some younger waitresses who care about their job and try to do their best. For those who want to learn, Sammi will take the time to teach them. They call her "Mama." Sammi said, "If

CAROL JIMENEZ SQUEEZING
BUTTER, SEARS FINE FOOD,
SAN FRANCISCO, CALIFORNIA

(LEFT) BRIT MESCHNARK,
HENDERSON, NEVADA

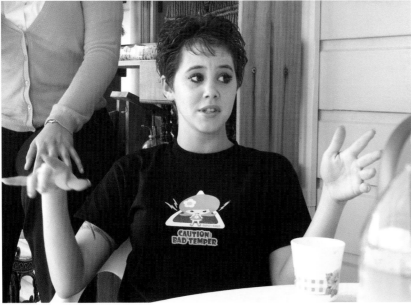

you explain to them why things should be done a certain way, they will listen and then everything else seems to fall into place."

As young women, most lifers didn't think they would be waiting tables past retirement age. If a waitress is ever faced with choosing waitressing as a career, it's usually during her forties. The generation born in the 1920s and 30s didn't have this choice because they had limited expectations about their work life. Those in their forties or fifties who have waitressed for twenty or more years, sometimes called "mid-lifers," seemed to have a harder time accepting their fate. Although most said they had no regrets, many wondered if their lives would have been different if they had gotten a college degree or pursued a dream they had when they were younger.

Some middle-aged waitresses used euphemisms to describe their job, saying they enjoyed working in the "hospitality business" or that they were in the "culinary industry." Georgina Moore of Reno, Nevada, said, "It was hard when I hit forty and realized that this was it for me. I had to change my attitude."

Virginia Brandon
Rainbow | Henderson, Nevada

I was born in Littleton, Colorado. I've got eight sisters and three brothers. We were migratory farm workers. I worked in the fields from when I was a little kid until I was about fifteen years old. My father was what they called the "straw boss," because he was one of the only workers who could speak English. But we didn't get off easy. He made sure we worked harder than anybody else. We'd get up at daylight and work 'til about ten in the morning and take a couple of hours off when it was the hot part of the day and go back out again. To this day, I won't eat in a car, because it reminds me of when we used to have to sit under the truck in the shade and eat bologna sandwiches.

My first waitressing job was at Bradley's in Littleton. Not long after that I worked for a newspaper, and then I worked in the welfare office as an interpreter, but I didn't make any money, so I went back to waitressing because it paid better.

Later, when I lived in California, my husband and I had our own restaurant. After we got rid of it, my husband went to Sacramento to look for a cooking job and all they paid was two dollars an hour and we had eight kids, so that wasn't going to work. We heard there was a union in Las Vegas, so we moved and I've been here ever since.

As soon as my kids turned fifteen or sixteen, they were all working. Most of my kids worked with me at the Rainbow. They're all good workers, but they're still spoiled. They just think about the job differently, I guess. When I started working, you went to work whether you had a cold, whether you had your period, whether you had a headache—you went to work. And that's a big distinction I see with the kids now. When I cut my foot with a weed whacker, I still went in. They sent me home, but I never thought about not coming in. The only time I got sick was always on a Wednesday: my day off. The only time I took off of work was if somebody died. I think in the almost thirty years I was at the Rainbow, I was late maybe one time.

My knees ached for years and then one day I went to get up and I couldn't move so I had to retire a few years ago. I had arthritis in my knees and I had to have surgery. I really wish I hadn't quit. I was so bored when I first retired. It's better now because I keep busy. I take karate three times a week. I don't think I've ever been in better physical shape and I'm seventy-one.

SONDRA DUDLEY, BUTTER CREAM BAKERY & DINER, NAPA, CALIFORNIA

Sondra Dudley

Butter Cream Bakery & Diner | Napa, California

I started waitressing at the Butter Cream when I was sixteen. My worst moment was when I first started. I was nervous. We kept this soup on the grill and I was new and I wanted to be right on it. Well, I caught the soup ladle when I was walking by and I had soup all over the front of me. It was navy bean soup, I remember. It burned.

I got a job at another restaurant, but I came back here. This is home. I came here because my mom had worked here when she was younger; she was a waitress and a cook. My mom and dad were friends with Bobby and David Claus [the owners]. We're all basically like a family. I went to school with Barbara and Jerry [part of the Claus family]. I've known them since we were little kids. And if you want to know any stories happening in town, everybody comes to Butter Cream. You can sit at the counter and get an earful and find out everything about everybody.

I know someday I'll be on Broadway. I just know it. I've taken tap dance for five years. And every day I go I say, "Please, God, make me get this." I think everybody has their dreams, but I'm very satisfied with my life. I love my job and I'm *happily* married. I'm one of the few people who can say that. My husband was a racecar driver for twenty years. We traveled the circuit. He won three championships. At that time, we didn't do much but race, we had a fun life—a gypsy life.

You never know what you're going to get with waitressing. You have the great people who come in and are really nice to you, and then you have the people who treat you badly and think you have to be here and that you have to wait on them. I don't *have* to be here. I'm here because I *want* to be here. My husband makes a good living so I don't have to come to work every day if I don't want to. And I'm very upfront with them. I tell them, "Be nice to me and I'll be nice to you. But don't do that mean stuff to me because I don't do it very well." When people get hostile, I just try to calm them down and say, "We can make things right if you want to. We can do this together" [laughing]. But then there are those people you can't satisfy no matter what. I believe that we make our own misery. I try to just have good vibes and I tell them, "Don't you pop my bubble. I'm in a good mood today."

I just come to work no matter what. One time at New Years I bought a treadmill. I was trying to get fit for the year and I slid and fell off the treadmill and came to work. I was all bruised up, but I was determined to make it. I could hardly breathe because I had a cracked rib, but I came to work. I would have stayed until Lexi [the manager] told me to go home.

You can have hard days. Sometimes it's jam-packed in here, and we are going from the time they open the doors until we close, and you're exhausted. But you go home, rest up, and come back. If my body holds out, I want to be waitressing for a long time. My feet [laughing], they hurt the worst. I guess I've complained about them enough. The people here got together and bought me a foot massager. My mother is eighty-six years old and she still works. And my grandmother lived to be ninety-three, and she worked all the time too. I don't plan on leaving here so, I hope I've got those good genes.

RIVERS COLEMAN, CRYSTAL GRILL, GREENWOOD, MISSISSIPPI

Rivers Coleman

Crystal Grill | Greenwood, Mississippi

I grew up on a farm picking cotton in Cascilla, Mississippi. It was a little old hick town. My parents were sharecroppers. We didn't have nothing so you had to work. Most people didn't have anything back then. The way I was raised, we didn't believe in sittin' around doin' nothing. They found something for you to do and you worked all the time.

I come here in 1959. I worked the breakfast shift for twenty-five years. I worked six days a week until last year and then I started cutting down. I am eighty years old now. I used to work seven days a week. I never really took any time off. When I had cancer of the uterus I was out for three weeks.

Now we use computers. Don't think that wasn't hard. I'm not that great with the computer. We have a new program now and I'm not used to it. I get so mad. I said I was going to quit. Now the young ones are good with these computers—they help me, if I get tangled up. Even though I'm eighty, I'm still learning a lot of things.

I start at 10 am and I get off at 10 pm. I go home for a few hours in the middle of the day to rest. I go home and lay down just a little and then I can come back and I'm okay. I used to work straight through. I can't do it anymore. It kills my legs.

In 1965, this place decided to become a club [for whites only]. It wasn't that they minded waitin' on 'em [blacks]. I mean, we have a lot of them [blacks] now, but we didn't used to. You had to have a key to come in that door. I think they just thought . . . well, you know how the people are in the South. I don't have to tell you. I've seen a lot down here. A few of the white customers, I'm not going to call no names. Anyway, there was this big tall fella and a colored boy come out and got him a cup a coffee and got him some sugar out of the sugar bowl, and he slapped him across the face. I didn't believe it. . . . Nobody should be treated this way. It made me so mad. But I think the South is beyond that now. I hope so. I think people should be able to go anywhere they want to in the world. I've always believed that. It was time for it to stop. Well, look who got elected last night [Barack Obama in the primary election]. Well, he's not elected yet, but he did so well . . . I hope he gets elected. It will make the change complete. We've come a long way [tears in her eyes].

I've never thought about doing anything else. Well I don't have a good education, and I don't want to work in no factory. But waitressing is a good, honest living. And nobody should be ashamed to do it. I was just always so thankful that I could make a living and take care of my kids. I was proud of the work. But I don't think you'll find that with the younger ones today. I doubt if they'll stay.

I've waitressed at least fifty-five years. I've done it so long I guess it's a habit. Last year I said I was going to quit and then this year I said I was going to quit and when the time comes, I just can't give it up. So as long as I'm able to work, I guess I'll work. Some of my customers say they won't come if I'm not here. I have friends in here, but not that many on the outside who amount to nothing, because they're not able to work anymore. You can't live if you don't work.

CRYSTAL GRILL, GREENWOOD, MISSISSIPPI

Refusing to Retire

Aging is one of the most daunting realities we face. Tasks that once could be accomplished with minimal effort become increasingly difficult. When waitresses go through menopause, they have to get creative to find relief. Maddee Curran, who at fifty-five has waitressed most of her life, said, "My hot flashes tend to get worse the busier we are (that's when the walk-in freezers become your pal)."

Although the physical and mental demands of waitressing can be grueling (even to the young), as waitresses age, they believe that the work is actually keeping their body healthy instead of wearing it down. Memorizing orders

prevents their minds from becoming lazy and forgetful. Older waitresses tend to look much younger than their actual years—they are models of healthy aging. Sammi DeAngelis of East Brunswick, New Jersey, said, "This job keeps me in shape. You're always running.

MAYE ELMORE,
GEORGE J'S,
GLASGOW, KENTUCKY

It's like you're in perpetual motion." Waitressing offers similar benefits of going to a gym. In an eight-hour shift the average waitress walks eight miles. She gets her cardio during the lunch rush, and carrying plates is similar to weight resistance training, which strengthens her bones and makes her less prone to breakage and osteoporosis. Linda Exeler of the Colonial Cottage in Erlanger, Kentucky, said, "The physical workout is great. I'm the same size now that I was when I started waiting tables."

Coffee shops are not the safest places to walk. The hustle of getting drinks to the table can cause liquids to slosh over the rim of the glass and onto the floor. So it's common for waitresses to spill drinks without even knowing it. And since most people are not looking at the floor when they walk, they can easily hit a wet spot and slip and fall. Although bussers are trained to wipe up spills immediately, it doesn't always happen quickly enough. And many coffee shops don't even have bussers, so small spills sometimes go unnoticed. "I've slipped in here so many times," said Juanita Bernard of Lexington, Kentucky. "But I just bounce right back up and keep on going. One of these days, I'm going to fall and I won't ever get up. I fell one day in here—it was morning and we had a carpet running from the kitchen door. One of the runners had pushed up the rug and I didn't know it, and here I come with a case of eggs and there I went. They all flew up and one went all the way over the camera hanging up in the corner. I bounced right back up. They said, "Juanita, you all right?" I said, "I reckoned. I ain't got no broken bones so I'm fine, but I broke a case of eggs."

JUANITA BERNARD, MEADOWTHORPE CAFE, LEXINGTON, KENTUCKY

Doctors say that exercise is the best medicine for arthritis. When people with arthritis sit, their joints stiffen and pain sets in. Waitressing forces a woman to move. Walking, bending, lifting, and carrying lubricates practically every joint in her body. Ina Kapitan, an eighty-three-year-old waitress in Florence, Massachusetts, said, "If I didn't wait tables, my arthritis would cripple me." Another New England waitress, Edie Shrage of Somerville, Massachusetts, has pain in her legs. "It's probably arthritis," she said "But even the young people complain about their legs. I have a lot of upper body strength. . . I'm in pretty good shape, considering. I know if I stayed home, I'd probably be sitting in a chair, watching TV, or reading. I wouldn't be doing anything physical. That's part of the reason why I work."

Despite the positive aspects of being physical at work, over the years, the job takes a toll on their bodies. When the pain gets to be too much, Ina said, "You just don't focus on the pain. If you think about it, it just makes it worse." Angel Stam of San Francisco admits the shoulder she has used to pour coffee is starting to "kill" her. And Sammi has three discs disintegrating in her spine. She said, "Some days I can barely move. But I still go to work, no matter what. I'm a pro, that's what you do."

For most veteran waitress, retirement is not an option. Career waitresses leave only when they physically can't work anymore. Either they are hospitalized for serious ailments such as cancer (probably from years of working in smoke-filled restaurants) or they are suffering from a crippling condition such as rheumatoid arthritis. The thought of sitting at home (often times alone), and doing nothing is a slow form of death for these women. When some waitresses leave the business, they believe it marks the beginning of the end of their lives.

Carol Jimenez of San Francisco said, "What am I going to do if I retire, sit at home and watch soap operas?" When Virginia Brandon retired at the age of sixty-two, she said, "My boss told me, 'Don't retire. Take a month off.' So about two weeks later he called me and asked, 'So how you doing?' and I said, 'I'm ready to go back to work.'"

Despite all the competition, the bickering and the melodrama among restaurant workers, it's hard for waitresses to leave a place that has become their home away from home. When Annie King broke her hip from slipping on ice in front of the Venus Diner in Gibsonia, Pennsylvania, she had to take time off. "Boy, that six months I was off was tough," she remembered. "After I could get around and I was allowed to drive, I'd come up to the diner every morning at five thirty and sit at the counter and have coffee and talk to everybody. I was so glad when I could finally get to get back to work."

Lifers will go to great lengths to keep working for as long as they can. They don't understand why people hassle them about choosing to work. Miss Roxie Burton of Washington, D.C., who is in her eighties, said, "Why should I stop when I don't want to and I feel alright? I feel better working than sitting at home." Ronnie Bello of Worcester, Massachusetts, said, "I never bring up my age with people because you'd be surprised how they look at you differently. I find that it's better if they don't know, so I don't tell anybody. Even my boss doesn't know because he'd probably say, "She's too old, she shouldn't be here."

When Laverne Phillips got laid off at the Seven Seas Restaurant in Sausalito, California, she thought it was probably because of her age. She was seventy-nine. When she applied for other waitressing jobs, no one was interested in hiring her. She said, "I know as soon as they saw my birth date on the application, they threw it in the trash. If they'd just meet me in person they would see that I can do the job. I don't feel anything like my age."

Jodell Kasmarsik of the Pie 'n Burger in Pasadena, California, said, "I don't plan on leaving. I'll be seventy in December [2005], but I can still outwork everyone in here. My boss was kidding with me the other day about my age and I said, 'Yeah, I'll be here in a wheelchair, still waiting tables.'"

For those waitresses who say retirement is not an option, some have managers who try to get them to slow down. Since 1969 Esther Paul has worked at Sharkey's for six, ten-hour days a week. When she turned seventy-five, Sharkey told the manager not to schedule Esther more than four days a week. Esther said, "Why? I can work, and I get so bored at home." Sharkey said, "Well, then you

ANNIE KING, VENUS DINER, GIBSONIA, PENNSYLVANIA

can come here and sit at the counter and talk to me, but you're not working."

Sharkey is selling his casino coffee shop and Esther is deeply concerned about the change. The new owners are boasting about their fancy, new slot machines and are modernizing the place with a face-lift; they want to bring Las Vegas to the small quiet town of Gardnerville, Nevada. The new owners have asked Esther to stay, but she said if they change it too much she may retire and volunteer at the senior center. Her regulars are terrified that Sharkey's will change into a place that won't fulfill the simple, basic needs

that Esther has for almost forty years. But this seems to be the direction that society is moving in. Replacing the old with the new is not only a way of life but a defining element of our culture. Things are changing so fast that we can barely get comfortable with what we have. This is true with everything from technology to home renovations. The barber Angel Delgadillo, who has been shaving beards on Route 66 since 1950 said, "We are losing yesterday fast. Today it's zap, zap, zap, get the money, get the next one, and go. Zap, there's your hamburger, zap, I've got your money. Next [shouting]! Well, the waitresses here in Seligman [Arizona] have time to talk to you.

There's no comparison. I don't mind shopping at K-Mart or the other chains . . . but what's still America is the small towns, hometown cafes, and hometown filling stations. It looks like yesterday and it feels like a part of yesterday and we are yesterday."

Although there will always be women who will wait tables their entire lives, will there always be lifers who love their jobs? Faye Blackwell of Washington, D.C., doesn't think so. "I think waitressing is simply going to be a means for girls to earn money to get through school or some crisis. I don't think society is geared toward this anymore. If you notice, you rarely see older servers today and a lot of that has to do with the restaurants: they want the young ones. They think that beauty attracts business and I know for a fact that it does not. People go to diners because they want to feel at home." Jodell agrees. "The younger generation will never truly appreciate waitressing," she said. "It's gone. It's just us older, war horses."

Not only will the waitresses change, but the customers will be different as well. Most career waitresses say that men make up 75 to 90 percent of their clientele. Many are widowed and don't know how to cook for themselves, so they rely on the diner for their meals and come in three times a day. As this generation of men pass away,

TEXACO, SELIGMAN, ARIZONA, 2001

PHIL TOMLIN, LOUIS' RESTAURANT, SAN FRANCISCO, CALIFORNIA

their sons will bring a new element of independence that their fathers didn't have. It's more likely that men of this younger generation will be single, either divorced or never married. In any case, they will probably know how to cook for themselves and will not go to a restaurant for every meal. As the decades pass, this new generation of customers will be very different from the typical regulars that waitresses serve today.

Once this subculture of older career waitresses is gone, who will take their place? Perhaps those who continue to wait tables and put in their time will be satisfied with their lives. But even if they accept their fate as a lifer, it's not likely that they will stay in the same restaurant for fifty or more years, since the average person today will have at least three careers in his or her lifetime and will often move away from their hometown. If she happens to like the job, then she will probably be good at it. But if she's regretful about her life path and ends up waitressing as a last resort, resentment will inevitably creep in and show through her labored grin.

It's impossible to know what the future holds, but regardless we should recognize and appreciate these women while they're still here—catering to our quirks, delivering warm-ups, and serving comfort and companionship. Joanne Joseph at Al's in San Francisco said, "I'd just as soon die here. This is where I want it to end. It's our life's blood. It's our life. My granddaughter says, 'I've got ketchup in my veins.'"

MAYFAIR DINER, PHILADELPHIA, PENNSYLVANIA

(RIGHT) JOANNE JOSEPH WITH HER REGULAR, JUAN, AL'S GOOD FOOD CAFE, SAN FRANCISCO, CALIFORNIA

ESTHER PAUL, SHARKEY'S,
GARDNERVILLE, NEVADA.
COURTESY OF ESTHER PAUL.

Esther Paul

Sharkey's | Gardnerville, Nevada

Here at Sharkey's, on the seventh of January, we have what is known as a Serbian or Orthodox Christmas party. Last year we had about five thousand people and it's all free. The whole place is closed up at noon. We have goat, our traditional dinner, and ham and turkey. We have cold cuts, about seven different salads, wine, soft drinks, and we set up the whole counter. All the tables are pushed together with white table cloths, and people come in from all over and eat. They line up at two o'clock in the afternoon clear down the street. We start serving at four o'clock and usually end about midnight.

We have live entertainment and everything. Sharkey has done this for about thirty years. It probably costs him about fifteen thousand dollars. We serve buffet-style and everybody in town helps. The local people volunteer to serve food and the waitresses are not on the time card that day. It's our Christmas present to him. Now the restaurant is being sold and the new management wouldn't honor it, so it's sad for the community to see it go.

I started waitressing in 1943. I had gone into nursing training. And when I got married there wasn't enough money for it. I had already applied under the GI Bill. If you wanted to be a nurse, they would put you through school, but you had to give the government three years of your life afterwards. But they wouldn't take you if you were married.

I worked as a waitress so my husband could go to school. We had three kids and we were married twenty-six years and one day he came home, packed his bags, and left me for a younger woman. Everybody in the neighborhood knew about it but me. It was tough. I thought if you're married, you're married for life. I was brought up Catholic, so I was taught that everything should be in his name, that a woman should obey her husband, that he was the head of the household, and that his word was the law. But I got up to reading on things and realized that this isn't so. So after the divorce me, I took my seven hundred dollars . . . I had never been out of the state of Illinois and I had never driven any place really except around town, but I got into my little green and white Chevelle and drove west. I was forty-five years old and didn't know a soul, but I thought, hey, I've got the world by the ass. I've got my health, and I can work. I'm not lazy. I found a job at Sharkey's almost right away. It was 1969. And the money was so good at the time. I thought, wow, this is really neat. I do what I want and I don't have to answer to a man or anything. I thought, why should I anyway?

Some of the waitresses I work with will say, "I'm not waiting on so and so . . . they don't leave anything." I say, "If they leave you a dollar, it's a dollar more than you had when you walked in this door." They'll start out leaving a dollar and then after a year they'll ask to sit with you and start leaving two dollars or three dollars. After a while, it adds up. Some girls would rather have a five dollar bill than wait on five tables and make ten dollars. It's too much work for them. They'd rather take the easy way out. But when we get busy in here, you can't set up the tables fast enough and we make good money.

I like doing extras for my special customers. I have a regular who likes these certain kind of peppers that we have, and they're not always out front, but they are in the back, and I know where everything is. So when he comes in, I always make sure there's a little dish of those peppers on the table. And he doesn't like carrots in his salad, so I make sure there's no carrots in his salad. And he likes a little cup of soup next to his salad, so I just make him half a salad and a cup of soup, but he thinks that he's getting something extra. What he's really getting is part of his wife's salad, but he doesn't know the difference. It's just little things like that that keep 'em coming back.

I'm the oldest one here. I don't know too many people my age who work. A lot of the women around here have never worked. They just let a man take care of them, and when the man dies they don't know what to do with themselves. They go to the senior center here for lunch everyday and complain about how bad they feel. We have men who come in and their wives don't work. They say, "You're still working? Why aren't you retired?" I say, "Because I don't want to be retired." I mean they act like you're senile because you care to work. They say, "You shouldn't be workin' now." I say, "Well then, what should I be doing?" Sittin' at home watchin' the television? Well, that would drive me ape.

Elaine Reynoldson

Mojo's, Lakeview Lanes Bowling Alley | Sun City, Arizona

I was born in 1925, and I've waitressed for about forty years. My husband was a truck driver, so I had to go to work and make more money. I worked in a place that offered fine dining—they served cocktails and so forth—but the only thing is that there weren't any blondes or redheads; they only wanted brunettes. They thought blondes and redheads were too fast. But they hired me anyway and I worked there for six years.

Like a lot of waitresses, I got audited in the seventies. Because we were claiming 10 percent of our salary, we were only making seventy-five cents an hour or a dollar an hour. When were audited, they were going to put a lien on the house. I think we had to go to a loan company and borrow like a thousand dollars to pay it off.

I took an office job as a cashier/receptionist. I worked there for two and a half years and I just wasn't making enough money, or maybe I was getting itchy. In any case, I just wanted to wait tables again. So I went to work nights. I worked days in the office and then I worked three nights a week. Friday, Saturday, and then maybe one night a week. So I was working eight days a week. Then I had to

INA KAPITAN, FLORENCE DINER, FLORENCE, MASSACHUSETTS

make a decision. That's when I went to the Terrace Restaurant. I left there in 1976. They tore it down and put a CVS there. It was such a beautiful restaurant. I couldn't believe it.

Even though I'm over eighty, I'm doing really well. I clean my own house and I think waitressing is good for my physical health. I was having trouble with my hips and knees with arthritis, but I've been doing really good. I only take one pill and that's for arthritis.

I have a boyfriend. He's ninety and he's quite alert and healthy. We go ballroom dancing. It's so much fun. He doesn't want to marry me because his kids don't want him to remarry, and I don't know if I'd want to get married anyway. I like things just the way they are.

Ina Kapitan

Florence Diner | Florence, Massachusetts

I was born June 21, 1921. I've been working at the Florence Diner since 1969. This place is over sixty years old. Everything we serve here is fresh. We're known for our coleslaw. Our corned beef hash is made here. Most restaurants buy it in cans, but we don't. We have one person that comes in who lives in Worcester, about sixty miles away. Every time he passes he stops in and gets a couple of the corned beef hashes to take and cook at home. They've [the owner] made some changes here, closed off part of the restaurant and made it into a sports bar. The old grill and steam table is gone.

It used to be out front; now everything comes out of the kitchen. All the counter stools and the floor are new. It's different. It's all modernized now.

I started waitressing so I could spend more time with my kids. I started off making $1.20 or $1.10 an hour and back then you were lucky if you made $3 or $4 dollars a day in tips because the meal prices were so different. Today we only make about $2.75 or $2.70 an hour and you make it up in tips if you're lucky, and if you're not, you don't.

Everything is so much more expensive these days—gas, food, housing. . . . I need to keep working it seems just to pay my health insurance. I have Blue Cross and Blue Shield and I pay over $1,400 every three months for it. A lot of people are going to Canada to get their medicine. It' just too expensive. I had to get a shot for anemia and it was $900! It's ridiculous.

But you know, money isn't everything. We had one fellow that came in years back. He was an alcoholic. He won $20,000 in a lottery ticket and he came in to have a steak dinner. He was sitting there eating and he started gasping and I walked over just as he was falling off the stool. We had to call 911 because we thought he was dying. I think he got food lodged in his windpipe. He only lasted a few days and then he died. So that $20,000 he won in the lottery never helped him very much.

I've always had good respect from everybody. Even the new bosses have treated me with respect. Every night when we close some of the kids working here will say they've done all their side work and you go around and you find they haven't done their work. You get to the point where you just do it yourself. But sometimes if you speak up and say, "Hey, this isn't done" they'll hurry and do something. They're not all bad. And I'm there for them if they need me. Especially when the customers hit on the girls. I'll walk over and look at them and say, "Hey that's my daughter you're talking to, so watch it." And I'll walk away. I say that even though it wasn't my daughter. They don't know the difference.

I work a full shift (seven hours) five days a week. I worked six days a week for years. I guess I'll retire when the spirit says stop or unless my boss tells me I have to quit, but he probably won't. I think if you feel you can do it, then you should do it. When we're not busy, my boss is always telling me, "Why don't you sit down?" but I say, "No, if I stop, I'll get too stiff," so I just keep moving. I see people come in and they're only in their fifties and they're more decrepit than I am. And that's because they're sitting around and not doing anything. If you sit at home and become a couch potato, you hurt and get more crippled all the time. I know, because I have a lot of arthritis and I'm on medication for it, but when I have pains, I'll limp, but if I keep moving, then the first thing you know, the pain is gone. I don't take any pain pills except for Tylenol. A lot of nights I'm really tired. I sit at home in my recliner and take a little nap before I get up and go to bed. But I feel good at the end of the day because I know that I've done good days work. The doctors say, "I don't know what you're doing but keep doin' it."

Annie King

Venus Diner | Gibsonia, Pennsylvania

I've been waitressing since I was thirteen years old and I'm sixty-nine now. When I first started I was only planning on staying for six months. But I really liked it, so I stayed. I've been doing this for about fifty-six years. I tried doing other work, but I don't like to sit.

My first waitressing job was at this place called the Convict Inn. It's been gone a long time. The booths were like cells, and they had doors on them with bars and stuff. They were wooden, but they

looked like cells. It was neat. From there, I went to Howard Johnson's on the turnpike. I've been here at the Venus Diner for about forty-five years. That's a lot of walking . . . and a lot of carrying. I worked seven days a week for about ten years. The only days I had off was when we were closed. But it didn't bother me. I can honestly say there's never a day when I don't want to go to work.

I don't think I'd ever want to work in a fancy restaurant. That's not my type of people. These are my type of people here—in a diner. You can make so many friends here and the people are so

MISS ROXIE BURTON, FLORIDA AVENUE GRILL, WASHINGTON, D.C.

nice. Of course you can run into some real grouchy ones too. Some people will treat you like you're a little bit lower than them because you're a waitress, but I just ignore them.

I broke my hip last January. I was off for six months. I fell out here on the sidewalk. It was just one sheet of ice and I slid and fell and landed right on my hip and shattered it. While I was off I got cards from a lot of my customers and they came to see me in the hospital. But it was hard being away from the restaurant. That's why thinking about retirement is so hard. I would miss all of my customers so much.

Miss Roxie Burton

Florida Avenue Grill | Washington, D.C.

I grew up working on my father's farm in Virginia. We had thirty acres. We grew tobacco, corn, wheat, potatoes, cabbage, string beans, butter beans, and peas. We raised all our own chickens and we had cows, horses . . . everything.

I've been working in restaurants for forty-two years. I thought about doing other work, several times. I went to business school. At that time it was IBM keypunching, but it's computers now. I also took up sewing, but I always stayed with restaurant work. I ran my own restaurant for five years, but I couldn't get it going like I wanted to. Instead of making money, I kept having to pour my own money into it. So I thought it was time to bail out.

I'm eighty years old and I work about five to six days a week. People say I'm a fast waitress. Working here, you have to be quick—especially on the weekends, when it gets crowded. We have all types of people in here, a lot of cab drivers and bus drivers. You know, just regular people. Some of 'em have patience and some of 'em don't. But somehow or another we manage to deal with all of 'em. But this is a special diner. People come here for our soul food—we serve ham hock sandwiches, red eye gravy, chitterlings, greens, and cornbread. You can't find too many places like ours. We've been here for over sixty years.

FLORIDA AVENUE GRILL, WASHINGTON, D.C.

JUANITA BERNARD, MEADOWTHORPE CAFE, LEXINGTON, KENTUCKY

Juanita Bernard

Meadowthorpe Cafe | Lexington, Kentucky

I grew up in the mountains in Harlan County, Kentucky. My father was a coal miner and my mother's daddy was a coal miner. My mother died a diabetic and my father died too; my grandmother raised me. She was a deputy sheriff. She carried a gun, so you know I was raised up right. You don't sass them old women.

I'm from the country and I've done nothing but work all my life. My first waitressing job was in a cafeteria. I guess it just came to me naturally. I liked being around people. If I wasn't around people, I'd go crazy.

There's nothing I don't like about this job. You don't believe that do you? Well, it's true. After I lost my husband, I just dove my life into restaurant work. I ain't got time to take no vacations. I was working six days a week but I had to cut it down to four. I guess I'm getting too old [laughing]. But I can still work circles around everybody in here. When I get too busy I joke around and say, "I'm meetin' myself several times a day, you know, walking in circles, turning around so many times." I'll go up there and dip up some gravy and pork chops and then I'll go over to the stove and get the sauce for the meatloaf and serve it. By the time you turn around like that for about an hour or two, you're meetin' yourself.

This is just a home country place—all home cookin'. We get mostly elderly people in here, and during the daytime, we get the city and factory workers. A bunch of these men come through here, and maybe a few women will come through and cut up with me. I can hear 'em as soon as they open the door. Everybody calls me "Mom." Even the black people will come in and holler "Mom" to me.

It's fun in here. One time a regular said to me, "Hey, Juanita. You wanna go out on a date?" And I said, "I'm old enough to be your grandmother." He said, "Well, how old are you?" I said, "I'm gonna be seventy in December." He said, "No. That's okay. You're too old." I said [laughing], "I'll go out with you if you want me to." He said, "No, just forget it."

It's been two weeks since I quit smoking and I'm about to go nuts. So I go around with a sucker in my mouth, or chewing gum. They don't say nothin' to me about it because they know I'm trying to quit. One of my customers brought me a bag of suckers to try and help me.

I'm almost seventy and everybody says I don't look it. I guess

working on my feet all this time has helped. Restaurant work is my life. I tried to retire. I stayed gone for about seven months, but I got so depressed, I had to come back. I just couldn't handle it. I guess I'll stay here until I can't walk no more.

Waitresses and Other Interviewees

Alma Neuschwander, John Ascuaga's Nugget Casino, John's Oyster Bar, Sparks, Nevada

Alan Levins, Wilma's regular, Sears Fine Food, San Francisco, California

Andrew Colvin, Wilma's regular, Sears Fine Food, San Francisco, California

Angel Delgadillo, Seligman, Arizona

Angel Stam, Sears Fine Food, San Francisco, California

Annie King, Venus Diner, Gibsonia, Pennsylvania

Arthur "Medicine Man" Sweet, Iron Skillet Truck Stop, Kingman, Arizona

Betty A. Murphy, Mastoris Diner, Bordentown, New Jersey

Bo Links, Wilma's regular, Sears Fine Food, San Francisco, California

Brenda Hirst, Silver Spoon, Kingman, Arizona

Brit Meschnark, Rainbow, Henderson, Nevada

Carol Jimenez, Sears Fine Food, San Francisco, California

Charlett Adams, Iron Skillet Truck Stop, Kingman, Arizona

Charlotte Solberg, Copper Cart, Seligman, Arizona

"Cheech" Kormos, Ed Dabevic's, Los Angeles, California

"Cowboy," Sip 'n Bite, Baltimore, Maryland

David and Doris Levitch, Maria's regulars, Louisville, Kentucky

David and Henrida Holloways, Maria's regulars, Louisville, Kentucky

Dolores Jeanpierre, Ole's Waffle Shop, Alameda, California

Dolores Stuart, Mayfair Diner, Philadelphia, Pennsylvania

Edith Schrage, Mt Vernon Restaurant, Somerville, Massachusetts

Elaine Reynoldson, Mojo's, Lakeview Lanes, Sun City, Arizona

Ellen Warren-Seaton, USA Country Diner, Windsor, New Jersey

Esther Paul, Sharkey's, Gardnerville, Nevada

Eunice Ramsey, Tastee Diner, Silver Springs, Maryland

Faye Blackwell, Trio Restaurant, Washington, D.C.

Fernanda Osborn, Copper Cart, Seligman, Arizona

Georgina Moore, Gold 'n Silver, Reno, Nevada

Geraldine Spinelli, Melrose Diner, Philadelphia, Pennsylvania

Ina Kapitan, Florence Diner, Florence, Massachusetts

Jackie Robinson, Busy Bee Cafe, Atlanta, Georgia

Jane Droukis, Agawam Diner, Rowley, Massachusetts

Jean Joseph, Al's Good Food Cafe, San Francisco, California

Jo Ann Archer, Crystal Diner, Lawrenceville, New Jersey

Joanne Joseph, Al's Good Food Cafe, San Francisco, California

Jodell Kasmarsik, Pie 'n Burger, Pasadena, California

Joe Ballard, Sears Fine Food, San Francisco, California

José Cerda, regular at Ole's Waffle Shop, Alameda, California

Jose Meservey, regular at Al's Good Food Cafe, San Francisco, California

Joyce Widmann, Crystal Diner, Lawrenceville, New Jersey

137

Juanita Bernard, Meadowthorpe Diner, Lexington, Kentucky

Karesse Klein, Sittons North Hollywood Diner, North Hollywood, California

Kathleen A. S. Woody, Ryan's, Florence, Alabama

Larry Mansbach, Wilma's regular, Sears Fine Food, San Francisco, California

Laverne Phillips, Seven Seas, Sausalito, California

Linda Exeler, Colonial Cottage, Erlanger, Kentucky

Lindsay Brandon, Rainbow, Henderson, Nevada

Mae Christmas, Edith's Cafe, Central City, Kentucky

Margaret Mansfield, regular at Ole's Waffle Shop, Alameda, California

Maria Terry, Churchill Downs Racetrack, Louisville, Kentucky

Martha McCall, Tastee Diner, Silver Springs, Maryland

Maye Elmore, George J's, Glasgow, Kentucky

Nicole Davey, Rainbow, Henderson, Nevada

Olesia Smith, Copper Cart, Seligman, Arizona

Pat Dermatis, Sip 'n Bite, Baltimore, Maryland

Paul Brandon, Rainbow, Henderson, Nevada

Paula Hazzouri, Buena Vista Cafe, San Francisco, California

Phil Tomlin, Louis' Restaurant, San Francisco, California

Rachel DeCarlo, Sittons North Hollywood Diner, North Hollywood, California

Rachel Lelchuk, Louis' Restaurant, San Francisco, California

Renee E. Donati, Harry's Plaza Cafe, Santa Barbara, California

Rivers Coleman, Crystal Grill, Greenwood, Mississippi

R. J. Kerl, Mastoris Diner, Bordentown, New Jersey

Ronnie Bello, Boulevard Diner, Worcester, Massachusetts

Roxie Burton, Florida Avenue Grill, Washington, D.C.

Ruth Ann Jensen, John Ascuaga's Nugget Casino, John's Oyster Bar, Sparks, Nevada

Sallie Power, Miz Brown's Feed Bag, San Francisco, California

Sammi DeAngelis, Seville Diner, East Brunswick, New Jersey

Sharon Bruno, Betsy's Pancake House, New Orleans, California

Shirley Reed, Los Angeles, California

Shirley Smith, Coffee Mug, Elko, Nevada

Sondra Dudley, Butter Cream Bakery & Diner, Napa, California

Sue Hopkins, Sondra's regular, Butter Cream Bakery & Diner, Napa, California

Susan Thurmond, Rainbow, Henderson, Nevada

Tom Hontalas, Louis' Restaurant, San Francisco, California

Virginia Brandon, Rainbow, Henderson, Nevada

Walter A. Baker, regular at George J's, Glasgow, Kentucky

Wilma Mobbs, Sears Fine Food, San Francisco, California

Sources

CHAPTER 1

Leon Elder and Lin Rolens, *Waitress: America's Unsung Heroine* (Santa Barbara: Capra Press, 1985), 8.

CHAPTER 2

History of diners and creation of a female-friendly environment: Richard J. S. Gutman, *American Diner: Then and Now* (Baltimore: The Johns Hopkins University Press, 1993), 84–91, and Andrew Hurley, *Diners, Bowling Alleys, and Trailer Parks: Chasing the American Dream in Postwar Consumer Culture* (New York: Basic Books, 2001), 26–58.

CHAPTER 3

Paul Montagna, *Occupations and Society: Toward a Sociology of the Labor Market* (New York: John Wiley, 1997).

"Emotional labor," a term coined by Arlie Hochschild: Greta Foff Paules, *Dishing It Out: Power and Resistance among Waitresses in a New Jersey Restaurant* (Philadelphia: Temple University Press, 1991), 161.

William Foote Whyte quotation: Dorothy Sue Cobble, *Dishing It Out: Waitresses and Their Unions in the Twentieth Century* (Chicago: University of Illinois Press, 1991), 47.

CHAPTER 5

Back of the house versus front of the house discussion: Erving Goffman, *The Presentation of Self in Everyday Life* (Garden City, NY: Doubleday Anchor, 1959), 19.

CHAPTER 6

Family Feud quotation: Debra Ginsberg, *Waiting: The True Confessions of a Waitress* (New York: Harper Collins, 2000), 112.

Harvey Girl history: Lesley Poling-Kemps, *The Harvey Girls: Women Who Opened the West* (Paragon House: New York, 1989).

Elbert Hubbard quotation: Poling-Kemps, *Harvey Girls*, 40b.

Hasher quotation: "No Hashers: Waitresses Now Must Have Tact and Charm and Apply Their Psychology," *Literary Digest*, May 1, 1937, 26–27.

James West quotation: Greta Foff Paules, *Dishing It Out: Power and Resistance among Waitresses in a New Jersey Restaurant* (Philadelphia: Temple University Press, 1991), 103.

Barry Blackman statement: Paules, *Dishing It Out*, 103.

William Foote Whyte quotation: William Foote Whyte, "When Workers and Customers Meet," in *Industry and Society*, ed. Whyte (New York: McGraw-Hill, 1946), 132–33.

CHAPTER 7

History of tipping: Greta Foff Paules, *Dishing It Out: Power and Resistance among Waitresses in a New Jersey Restaurant* (Philadelphia: Temple University Press, 1991), 42–43, and Debra Ginsberg, *Waiting: The True Confessions of a Waitress* (New York: Harper Collins, 2000), 28–39.

Waitresses and divorce: Frances Donovan, *The Woman Who Waits* (Boston: Gorham Press, 1920).

Wage information from the Bureau of Labor Statistics website.

CHAPTER 8

Generational discussion: Ron Zemke, Claire Raines, and Bob Filipczak, *Generations at Work: Managing the Clash of Veterans, Boomers, Xers, and Nexters in Your Workplace* (New York: Amacom American Management Association, 2000); Jeffrey Arnett, quoted in "Quarterlife Crisis Hits Many in Late 20s: Settling on a Real, Grown-Up Job Is Harder for a New Generation of College Grads" by Keturah Gray, April 21, 2005, ABC News.com.

"Quarterlife crisis": Alexandra Robbins and Abby Wilner, *Quarterlife Crisis: The Unique Challenges of Life in Your Twenties* (New York: J. P. Tarcher, 2001).

Corante is an unbiased source on technology, business, law, science, and culture and produces conferences and publications on work and technology.

Education statistics: U.S. Census Bureau website, U.S. Department of Education.

Bibliography

Baeder, John. *Diners*. New York: Harry N. Abrams, 1978.

———. *Gas Food and Lodging: A Postcard Odyssey through the Great American Roadside*. New York: Abbeville Press, 1982.

Bartky, Sandra Lee. *Femininity and Domination: Studies in the Phenomenology of Oppression*. New York: Routledge, 1990.

Behar, Ruth, and Deborah A. Gordon. *Women Writing Culture*. Berkeley and Los Angeles: University of California Press, 1995.

Berger, John. *Ways of Seeing*. London: Penguin, 1972.

Boynton, Robert S. *The New New Journalism: Conversations with America's Best Nonfiction Writers on the Craft*. New York: Vintage, 2005.

Burgin, Victor. *In Different Spaces: Place and Memory in Visual Culture*. Berkeley and Los Angeles: University of California Press, 1996.

Clifford, James. *Routes*. Cambridge: Harvard University Press, 1991.

Clifford, James, and George E. Marcus. *Writing Culture: The Poetics and Politics of Ethnography*. Berkeley and Los Angeles: University of California Press, 1986.

Cobble, Dorothy Sue. *Dishing It Out: Waitresses and Their Unions in the Twentieth Century*. Chicago: University of Illinois Press, 1991.

Davis, Angela Y. *Women, Race & Class*. New York: Vintage, 1981.

Donovan, Frances. *The Woman Who Waits*. Boston: Gorham Press, 1920.

Ehrenreich, Barbara. *Nickel and Dimed: On (Not) Getting By in America*. New York: Metropolitan/Owl Books, 2001.

Elder, Leon, and Lin Rolens. *Waitress: America's Unsung Heroine*. Santa Barbara: Capra Press, 1985.

Ewen, Stuart. *All Consuming Images: The Politics of Style in Contemporary Culture*. New York: Basic Books, 1988.

Foucault, Michel. *Discipline and Punish*. Trans. A. M. Sheridan-Smith. Harmondsworth: Penguin, 1977.

Genovese, Peter. *Jersey Diners*. New Jersey: Rutgers University Press, 1997.

Ginsberg, Debra. *Waiting: The True Confessions of a Waitress*. New York: Harper Collins, 2000.

Goffman, Erving. *The Presentation of Self in Everyday Life*. Garden City, NY: Doubleday Anchor, 1959.

Gutman, Richard J. S. *American Diner: Then and Now*. Baltimore: The Johns Hopkins University Press, 1993.

Hess, Alan. *Googie: Redux Ultramodern Roadside Architecture*. San Francisco: Chronicle Books, 2004.

Hochschild, Arlie. *The Managed Heart: Commercialization of Human Feeling*. Berkeley and Los Angeles: University of California Press, 1983.

hooks, bell. *Where We Stand: Class Matters*. New York: Routledge, 2000.

Hurley, Andrew. *Diners, Bowling Alleys, and Trailer Parks: Chasing the American Dream in Postwar Consumer Culture*. New York: Basic Books, 2001.

Isay, David, and Harvey Wang. *Holding On: Dreamers, Visionaries, Eccentrics, and Other American Heroes*. New York: W. W. Norton, 1996.

Kessler-Harris, Alice. *Out to Work: A History of Wage-Earning Women in the United States.* Oxford: Oxford University Press, 2003.

Landlay, Lori. *Madcaps, Screwballs and Con Women: The Female Trickster in American Culture.* Philadelphia: University of Pennsylvania Press, 1998.

Langdon, Philip. *Orange Roofs, Golden Arches: The Architecture of American Chain Restaurants.* New York: Knopf 1986.

Lupton, Ellen. *Mechanical Brides: Women and Machines from Office to Home.* New York: Cooper-Hewitt and Princeton Architectural Press, 1993.

Lupton, Ellen, and J. Abbott Miller. *Hygiene, Cuisine and the Product World of Early Twentieth-Century America.* New York: Zone, 1992.

Montagna, Paul D. *Occupations and Society: Toward a Sociology of the Labor Market.* New York: John Wiley, 1997.

"No Hashers: Waitresses Now Must Have Tact and Charm." *Literary Digest.* May 1, 1937, 26–27.

Owings, Alison. *Hey, Waitress! The USA from the Other Side of the Tray.* Berkeley and Los Angeles: University of California Press, 2002.

Paules, Greta Foff. *Dishing It Out: Power and Resistance among Waitresses in a New Jersey Restaurant.* Philadelphia: Temple University Press, 1991.

Poling-Kemps, Lesley. *The Harvey Girls: Women Who Opened the West.* Paragon House: New York, 1989.

Polster, Bernd, and Phil Patton. *Highway: America's Endless Dream.* New York: Stewart, Tabori and Chang, 1997.

Potter, David M. *People of Plenty: Economic Abundance and the American Character.* Chicago: University of Chicago Press, 1954.

Robbins, Alexandra, and Abby Wilner. *Quarterlife Crisis: The Unique Challenges of Life in Your Twenties.* New York: J. P. Tarcher, 2001.

Rose, Mike. *The Mind at Work: Valuing the Intelligence of the American Worker.* New York: Viking, 2004.

Spain, Daphne. *Gendered Spaces.* Chapel Hill: University of North Carolina Press, 1992.

Stern, Jane, and Michael Stern. *Eat Your Way Across the U.S.A.* New York: Broadway Books, 1999.

Stewart, Kathleen. *A Space on the Side of the Road: Cultural Poetics in an "Other" America.* Princeton: Princeton University Press, 1996.

Whyte, William Foote. *Industry and Society.* Edited by William Foote Whyte. New York: McGraw-Hill, 1946.

Willis, Paul. *The Ethnographic Imagination.* Malden, MA: Blackwell, 2000.

Zemke, Ron, Claire Raines, and Bob Filipczak. *Generations at Work: Managing the Clash of Veterans, Boomers, Xers, and Nexters in Your Workplace.* New York: Amacom American Management Association, 2000.